Praise for *Your To-Die-For Life*

"Who knew trauma and death could be so inspirational?"
—Jenny Lawson, #1 *New York Times* bestselling author of *Furiously Happy*

"What I love most about *Your To-Die-For Life* is how Karen transforms our greatest fear into our greatest teacher. This book isn't just about preparing for death—it's about keeping the end in mind in order to truly live. A must-read for anyone seeking a more meaningful life."
—Kristine Carlson, *New York Times* bestselling coauthor of the Don't Sweat the Small Stuff book series

"Life is precious, and Karen Salmansohn's *Your To-Die-For Life* is a powerful reminder of just that. Instead of fearing mortality, this book challenges us to use it as fuel—to stop waiting, start living, and focus on what truly matters. With eye-opening insights and practical wisdom, Karen helps us shift our perspective, embrace each day with purpose, and create a life we won't regret. If you've been caught up in the busyness of life, consider this your wake-up call."
—Mark and Angel Chernoff, *New York Times* bestselling coauthors of *Getting Back to Happy*

"*Your To-Die-For Life* is the perfect how-to guide for those of us who yearn for deeper meaning but often find ourselves lost in a blur of screens and mundane tasks. Karen's wise, witty voice and her research-based advice remind us: 'Yes, I was here. I lived fully. I paid attention.' Don't miss out on your life, or this book!"
—Nanea Hoffman, founder of Sweatpants & Coffee

"I love Karen Salmansohn. She knows exactly what to say to help me wake up and LIVE. In *Your To-Die-For Life*, she made me laugh out loud while delivering profound truths I find so easy to forget or discount. This book pushed me out of a rut and back toward finishing my novel when I wanted to give up. It's soothing and challenging, a rare mix that was exactly what I needed! Read this if you find yourself needing a nudge to keep going after your dreams!"
—Jen Louden, author of *Why Bother: Discover the Desire for What's Next*

"As someone who's all about breaking rules and challenging status quos, I'm totally here for Karen Salmansohn's *Your To-Die-For Life*. This isn't just another self-help book—it's a manifesto for those ready to design a life that's as unique and powerful as they are. It's raw, it's real, and it'll light a fire under your tush to start living authentically."

—Esther Blum, RDN, CDN, CNS, menopause expert and author of *See ya later, Ovulator!*

"Death is inevitable—why not make it your life coach? With wit, wisdom, and wildly practical advice, this book flips the script on mortality, turning it into your ultimate catalyst for joy, purpose, and a damn good life. Fun, unexpected, and seriously life-changing!"

—Arielle Ford, author of *The Love Thief*

"With wisdom, wit, and a dose of irreverence, *Your To-Die-For Life* by Karen Salmansohn challenges you to confront your life's what-ifs and why-nots. The insights and actionable steps in this book can serve as a loving kick in the butt to help readers embrace the life they want."

—Andrea Syrtash, founder and editor-in-chief of *Pregnantish*

"Karen Salmansohn's *Your To-Die-For Life* is a powerful and uplifting book that reframes the often-taboo topic of mortality into an inspiring, wisdom-filled conversation infused with light humor. This book encourages you to embrace the fragility of life as a catalyst for creating a life rich in happiness, purpose, and fulfillment."

—Dana-Maxx Pomerantz, founder of The Be Happy Project

"Karen's book focuses beautifully on one of my favorite topics: how to stay alive inside of life. Let this experienced guide walk with you toward greater depth and joy in your life."

—Jacob Nordby, creative coach and author of *The Creative Cure*

"*Your To-Die-For Life* is not about dying—it's about living with the volume turned up, filters turned off, and fears turned down. Karen Salmansohn writes as if life itself depends on it, because, well, it does. A powerful reminder that contemplating death can be the ultimate motivation to live more carefully and deeply."

—Susan Shapiro, author of *The Forgiveness Tour*

"This isn't just another self-help book—it's a wake-up call wrapped in wisdom, humor, and profound truth. Karen Salmansohn takes the taboo topic of death and transforms it into an inspiring guide for living. *Your To-Die-For Life* offers exactly what our busy, distracted world needs: a reminder that our time is precious and now is the time to start living like we know it."

—Lori Deschene, founder of Tiny Buddha
and author of Tiny Buddha's Gratitude Journal

"Ideally we all want to live a life without regret, but the process to get there and maintain that involves incredible self-growth, focus, and the ability to share our purpose with others. *Your To-Die-For Life* teaches us all the values to live with and by *now* so when we have shuffled off this mortal coil we know those around us shared in that purpose and joy when it mattered the most."

—David Homan, CEO of Orchestrated Connecting

"I love the wisdom and inspiration Karen shares with her warm voice and signature sassy wit that will coax you to go for it! If not now, when?! I'm living proof that it's never too late to pursue a passion and embrace your time here, if you make it a priority."

—Robin Gorman Newman, Tony Award–winning Broadway producer
and author of How to Marry a Mensch

"If life's a journey, *Your To-Die-For Life* is the cheeky road map showing you where to stop for fantastic views and how to avoid bumps along the way. Karen Salmansohn delivers her strategies for fully embracing our finite lives with an empowering combo of humor and poignancy."

—Stella Grizont, national bestselling author of The Work Happiness Method

"*Your To-Die-For Life* isn't just a book—it's a powerful interruption to the autopilot existence we sometimes find ourselves in. Karen Salmansohn doesn't sugarcoat or sidestep; she speaks straight to the part of you that knows there's more and won't settle for anything less. This isn't about someday—it's about now. Every page is a push, a wake-up call, a challenge wrapped in love. It's like sitting down with the boldest, most unstoppable version of yourself and getting real about what you're here to create. If you're ready to stop waiting and start fully living, this book is your moment."

—Josselyne Herman-Saccio, master coach and vision architect

"Life isn't meant to be endured—it's meant to be savored, celebrated, and occasionally turned upside down just to see what falls out of its pockets. *Your To-Die-For Life* will help you to do just that! Through powerful practices and insightful perspectives on your mortality, you'll learn to create a life that feels less like a should-do list and more like a love letter to yourself."

—Lisa McCourt, author of Free Your Joy: The Twelve Keys to Sustainable Happiness

"In such a beautiful way, Karen weaves humor and deep care with creativity, passion, and credibility. It's absolutely outstanding. Reading this book gives you the feeling of a beautiful roller-coaster ride of awareness, curiosity, education, fun, and so much more! Thank you, Karen, for bridging this topic with such grace and ease."

—Adam Gaskill, CEO and founder of The Nonprofit Creators and Innovate for Humanity

"Karen Salmansohn presents a compelling case for making peace with our mortality in *Your To-Die-For Life*. Each chapter is a stepping stone toward a life lived with less fear and more bravery, love, purpose, and meaning."

—Meri Frischman, founder of The Proage Woman

"In *Your To-Die-For Life*, Karen Salmansohn reminds us that mortality isn't just the dark shadow we might believe it to be. It's a light illuminating every precious moment. Like a compass pointing true north, this book guides us toward living with intention rather than inertia."

—Skylar Liberty Rose, pro-aging advocate

"I'm fluent in the language of empowerment, and *Your To-Die-For Life* speaks directly to my soul! Leave it to ever clever Karen Salmansohn to turn a scary idea into the jet fuel required to get off autopilot and craft instead—day by day, moment by moment—a life bursting with authenticity, meaning, and joy. This 'get-to-living' guidebook is inspirational and actionable to the last word."

—Becky Vollmer, author of *You Are Not Stuck*

"This book offers more than wisdom . . . it offers a path to self-discovery. Karen's insights help us navigate our lives with greater mindfulness, making each moment count in a profoundly meaningful way. A must-read for anyone looking to deepen their connection to themselves and the world around them."

—Steve Stein, publisher and founder of BetterListen and WisdomFeed

""Karen Salmansohn's *Your To-Die-For Life* dares readers to embrace every messy, beautiful moment of life with courage and humor. It's a bold, heartfelt reminder that true living begins where fear of the inevitable ends."

—Karen Giberson, president and CEO of the Accessories Council

"This is not only the funniest book about death I've ever read, it's also an inspiring, useful guide for living with greater joy and purpose . . . and less fear and regret."

—AJ Jacobs, New York Times bestselling author of *The Year of Living Constitutionally*

YOUR
to-die-for
LIFE

Also by Karen Salmansohn

How to Be Happy, Dammit
The Bounce Back Book
Prince Harming Syndrome
Enough, Dammit
Think Happy
The 7 Lively Sins
Instant Calm
Life Is Long
Happy Habits
Listen to Your Heart Line-a-Day Journal
Instant Happy Journal

YOUR
to-die-for
LIFE

How to maximize joy and minimize regret... before your time runs out

KAREN SALMANSOHN

BenBella Books, Inc.
Dallas, TX

BenBella Books, Inc.
8080 N. Central Expressway
Suite 1700
Dallas, TX 75206
benbellabooks.com
Send feedback to feedback@benbellabooks.com

BenBella is a federally registered trademark.

Printed in the United States of America
10 9 8 7 6 5 4 3 2 1

Library of Congress Control Number: 2025001597
ISBN 9781637747025 (trade paperback)
ISBN 9781637747032 (electronic)

Editing by Rick Chillot
Copyediting by Scott Calamar
Proofreading by Jenny Bridges and Marissa Wold Urhina
Text design and composition by Jordan Koluch
Printed by Lake Book Manufacturing

To my kind-hearted dad, who passed away far too soon, leaving behind the wake-up call that life is too precious to sleep through. To my inspiring 90-something mom, who taught me that you don't have to slow down at a certain age . . . just because the world tells you to. To my awesome son Ari, who's the reason I'm considering living forever . . . or at least as long as I can continue to embarrass him. And to my highly appreciated Howard, my sidekick in this adventure, who's always making sure life is far more enjoyable.

Contents

Introduction:
Are You Having a Near-Life Experience?

So, here's the thing: I didn't write this book about death because I had some near-death experience. There was no tunnel of light, no out-of-body moment where I floated above myself and thought, *"Wow, I really should have moisturized more."* None of that.

I'm writing this book because I experienced something far scarier:

A near-*life* experience.

Now, you're probably wondering, "What on earth is a near-life experience?"

Well, it's this thing that many of us do ... you know, where you're *technically* alive. You're here. Your heart's beating. Your lungs are doing their thing. But you're not *actually* living. You're just kind of ... life adjacent.

You're on autopilot.

You go through the motions—work, text, eat, sleep—but you're not fully present. You're phoning it in. Literally phoning it in, because you're on your phone too much.

You walk outside to get some fresh air, but you end up staring at your phone.

Then you refresh your phone's various apps and feeds—but you don't refresh yourself. Why? *Because it's easier to get caught up in other people's lives than it is to engage with your own.*

So you're alive, at least in the sense that you're not dead.

But you're constantly somewhere else mentally, checking out from the real world, because the virtual one on your screen is so tempting and convenient.

Or maybe you're not mesmerized by your phone ... *but you're still not fully present.*

- You're at your monthly book club. But while others are dissecting the author's themes, you're dissecting your last conversation with your teenager.
- You're at a family BBQ. But instead of tasting the burgers, you're chewing on the bitterness of some unresolved conflict.
- You're at dinner with a loved one. But while they're sharing heartfelt stories, your mind is replaying stressful emails from work.

These are what I call near-*life* experiences.

You're living, yes, but your life is diluted, watered down. You're showing up, but half the time . . . you could be replaced by a cardboard cutout, and no one would even notice.

And then there is that other type of near-life experience—the kind where you "nearly live" the life you want—but you keep putting off important things till "someday."

Some nearly lived moments:

- You plan to reconnect with old friends over dinner, but as the night approaches, you're overwhelmed by the energy it takes to be "on"—so you cancel.
- You think about returning to school to chase a deferred dream, but then you choke on the what-ifs of failing . . . or starting too late.
- You keep meaning to call your parents more often—but every time you think about it, you suddenly remember you need to clean something . . . immediately.
- You tell yourself that someday you will try something new . . . as soon as "new" stops being synonymous with "terrifying."

Let me tell you: Each of these near-life experiences is sneaky.

Often you don't realize you're having them until you've had too many to count. And most of us have had more than we'd like to admit.

As a result, many of us have trained ourselves to be comfortable with just . . . *enough.*

Just *enough* attention. Just *enough* effort. Just *enough* connection.

It's like we've collectively decided that being fully present in our lives is overrated.

The crazy part: Even when we know we're doing it, we just don't care. We've become so comfortable with being disconnected from our lives that we've convinced ourselves that this is normal.

We're like, "Eh, this is just how it is now. It's fine."

But it's not fine.

It's not even close to fine.

Living this way is like using a phone charger that's frayed and barely working, and thinking, "Well, it's not on fire yet, so it's fine."

But it's only a matter of time before it burns your house down.

The worst part?

Deep down, you know this isn't how you want to live your life. The whole time, there's this low-level anxiety humming in the background, whispering, "This isn't it. This isn't the life you were meant to live."

But instead of dealing with this whispered warning, you just turn up the volume on a podcast or scroll through Instagram, pretending you didn't hear it.

And that's why I'm writing this book.

I want to wake you up from your near-life experiences—snap you out of your autopilot slumber.

And I've got just the tool to do it:

DEATH AWARENESS

Yeah, I know, death isn't exactly a fun topic. But guess what? Thinking about death can ironically breathe new life into you. In fact . . .

Death awareness is a powerful life hack.

I found this out the hard way, when I lost my father about two decades ago.

Let me tell you: When death shows up, it does this thing. It taps you on the shoulder, and without saying a word, it lets you know that you've been wasting a lot of your time.

My father's death did this for me.

After my dad died I found myself thinking about the finite nature of my life. Soon after, I began reassessing my priorities, eager to live more intentionally, to cherish small moments more often, to express love more frequently.

It was as if I'd been living half asleep and someone finally slapped me awake. Suddenly my view of the life around me became sharper. I could see all the ridiculous clutter that filled my days—years' worth of bad habits and wasteful distractions. This kicked off a serious spring-cleaning of my priorities.

I began to break free from my near-life experience stupor.

BEFORE MY DAD PASSED...

I was living my life as if I had a thousand years ahead of me. Just coasting, putting off all the important stuff. Start a family? Nah, I'll do that later. Go on those dream trips? Eh, maybe next year. I thought there were always more tomorrows.

AFTER MY DAD DIED, IT HIT ME...

There *isn't* an infinite supply of tomorrows. Not for any of us.

I began to realize how fragile life is; it could break at any time. Life has a use-by date. It's not an endless scroll. You're here. Then you're not. And it's up to us to make the "here" part as meaningful as possible.

When you take the time to really sit with the fact that, sorry, *you're going to die someday—and that it could be sooner than you think*—it does something to you.

You stop living like you're gonna be here forever . . . and start recognizing that you're not.

CASE IN POINT FROM MY OWN LIFE...

Death, it turns out, is an excellent alarm clock. After my dad passed, I woke up to the idea of starting a family—a thought I'd been swatting away for years.

Suddenly, it became crystal clear. Although I was fulfilled by my career, I wanted more. I craved the whole family-sized love package—a home filled with laughter, sticky fingerprints, weird kid questions like "Why is air invisible?," and a loving partner (someone like my Howard) to share the chaos, joy, and crumbs with.

So I have my father's death to thank for my son Ari's birth. His passing cracked something open in me. That's what death awareness does.

On an interesting note:

My son was born exactly four years to the day of my dad's passing—on August 27th. It felt like kismet that my dad's "death day" was also my son's birthday. It felt like a wink from my dad, saying, *I'm happy for you, Karen.*

BUT HERE'S THE CRAZIEST PART

We all *know* that life is not forever.

We don't need someone to die to remind us that life is impermanent. The problem is: We don't like to think about the reality of death. So we act like we have all the time in the world to start living.

But once you accept that your time is limited, you stop treating every day like it's just another hurdle to get through. And you start treating your life like the finite, precious fleeting thing it is.

- You stop putting things off to someday—and become a choosier choice chooser about how you spend your time now.
- You start investing in relationships that truly matter—and activities that fulfill you.
- You start to see the beauty in mundane moments—a dog's wagging tail, the peculiar shape of a cloud, the lilting melody in a friend's laugh.
- You start to prefer to binge-watch the sunset over the latest Netflix series, because you understand that some things truly are limited editions.
- You begin to look at that big pile of laundry you're folding and think about how it represents lives being lived.
- And those dishes in your sink? They become a testament to food enjoyed and intimate conversation exchanged.
- Suddenly a hug from a loved one now feels like it could power a small city.

Yes, ironically, when you become death aware, you become a life enthusiast.

Skeptical? Guess what? I'm not the only one fan-girling death awareness. The perks of death awareness are plentiful and research based.

I know this for a fact—because I love collecting facts. You see, for the last few decades I've been a bestselling author of psychological and philosophical books, as well as a total research geek. Naturally, after the passing of my father, I became curious about why his death had sharpened my lens on life so greatly. So I went into research mode.

I quickly discovered a wide range of studies that preached the benefits of death awareness.

For example . . .

- **"Effects of mortality awareness." (Daniel Spitzenstätter and Tatjana Schnell).** This study demonstrated that thinking about death reduced people's fears of dying—and inspired them to live more bravely.
- **"How thinking about death can lead to a good life."** This study (published in *Society for Personality and Social Psychology*) reported that mulling over mortality motivates us to improve our lives. It's, like, walk past a graveyard, feel more inspired to do better and be better.
- **University of Missouri study on death reminders:** Apparently, thinking about kicking the bucket makes people less likely to reach for a cigarette or a beer.
- **"Greedy bastards" study:** This cheekily named research found that a nudge about our mortality turns us into people who are more about giving and less about grabbing.
- **Hirschberger, Florian, Mikulincer study on death reminders:** This study said that reminders of our eventual demise make us nicer. As in, *Hey, you're going to die one day. Now, go be kind!*

What does all of that mean?

Getting chummy with your mortality is not morbid. It's *motivating*.

Yes, the more you come to terms with your mortality, the more you'll live with *more* joy, not less. *More* purpose, not less. *More* exclamations of "Hell yeah!" Not less.

Death is indeed the ultimate life coach.

After digging into all this death-awareness research, I thought, *"Why not test this out with some mortality awareness tools?"*

So I did. I experimented with writing my own eulogy, crafting an epitaph for myself, scribbling daily "To-Die" lists to follow (which are really more like "What Actually Matters Most" lists).

Guess what? My life started to bloom in unexpected ways, both professionally and personally.

Naturally, I shared these mortality awareness tools with my clients, and they were blown away by the results. It was as if I'd handed them some strange, magical key. Suddenly they were unlocking doors to long-forgotten dreams and dusty ambitions that they'd almost given up on. Jobs were quit, businesses born, new countries explored, college degrees revisited, passions ignited.

Now I'm excited to awaken and empower you too!

I want to encourage you to use the fact that you're not immortal . . . as a *push-yourself-off-the-couch-and-into-the-world* button.

I want you to get cozier with the idea of your mortality—but not in a "hide under the blankets" way. Quite the opposite. I want you to use the fear of the end as fuel for the now.

Once you learn to embrace the undeniable fact that you're not gonna be here forever, you'll soon find that every decision, relationship, and leap becomes more infused with bravery, urgency, and passion.

After all, when you realize that every Netflix binge means making the choice against, say, writing your novel—or calling an old friend—or volunteering at the local animal shelter . . . *your priorities get a little shake-up.*

Sounds counterintuitive, right? Death as a positive motivator?

It's like finding out that Brussels sprouts are actually delicious when roasted just right. Surprising, but also totally true!

So, if you're tired of living *next to* your life instead of *in* it . . . stick around.

In the pages ahead, I will show you, step by simple step, how to use thoughts about the end of your life to make the beginning and middle far better.

And don't worry, I'm not saying you have to stop scrolling on your phone altogether. I'm not a monster.

My goal is to help you to find that sweet spot, where you unplug far more frequently from technology and connect more often to the most important people and passions in your life.

This book is meant to serve as a loving "speed bump" in the hectic rush of your life, encouraging you to take the time to ask yourself:

What truly matters most to me?

So when it comes right down to it, this book isn't about death at all. It's actually about how to live more fully.

To quote the brilliant philosopher Lucius Annaeus Seneca: "It is not that we have a short time to live, but that we waste a lot of it."

So let's not waste any more time. Let's embrace our mortality, and in so doing, let's embrace life like never before.

We might not have control over when or how we'll exit this world. But we do have control over how we live it now.

Death is inevitable. But a life lived with regret doesn't have to be.

WHY DEATH IS YOUR BEST KICK IN THE TUSH TO LIVE BETTER

Early in the morning, when I've just made coffee and the rest of the house is still lost in dreams, I think about dying. Not in a "curl up in the fetal position" way. But more like a "What the hell am I doing with my life?" way.

I call this a *Death Mindfulness Practice*.

And I know what you're thinking: Mindfulness + death? First thing in the morning? What, are you just trying to ruin your day?

But here's the thing: It works.

So, while everyone else is busy pretending they're going to live forever, I'm over here using death as a daily wake-up call. And it's very motivating.

I'll be sharing my exact Death Mindfulness Practices in the pages ahead. But for now please know: These practices are not the usual ho-hum sit-cross-legged-and-find-your-center kind of stuff you might do in yoga class that often makes you just want to fall asleep.

I would know, because I studied to be a yoga and meditation teacher.

Instead of calming you, these death mindfulness tools sharpen you. They're more like slap-you-in-the-face tools that get you to stop sleepwalking through your life and actually start paying attention.

Plus best of all: They're fun and easy to do.

I get it ...

At first, the idea of "fun death mindfulness tools" sounds a little nuts. Like, "What's so fun about starting my day thinking about dying?" It sounds like a bummer.

But here's the thing ...

When you start your day thinking, "Holy crap, I'm still here. I'm still alive. Let's go!," it's like flipping a switch. Suddenly, your whole day has this urgency to it, this weird sense of adventure. And instead of, "Why must I crawl out from under these warm, cozy blankets?" you're thinking, "What can I do with this extra bonus day the universe just handed me?"

It's funny, isn't it?

You focus on something as future based and morbid as death, and somehow it makes you feel more alive and happy, right now.

All of a sudden, every day is a little bit more vivid. It's as if you've been wearing the wrong prescription glasses your whole life, and you just got the right ones. Every little thing seems a bit more important, a bit more urgent, a bit more amazing.

YOU'RE MORTAL. QUIT DAWDLING.

Death Mindfulness is an effective tool because death is the ultimate deadline. And nothing, *I mean nothing*, makes a person more productive than a looming deadline. Especially one you can't negotiate your way out of.

You know how you feel when you realize you only have so many bites of your sandwich left, and you start savoring each bite more? You chew slower. Taste longer. Maybe even slather on more condiments. With daily death awareness, you start to savor your life like that.

Now, everybody's gonna die, right? But nobody wants to talk about it.

We'll talk about politics, religion, your cousin's messy divorce. But death? That's the conversational no-go zone.

I remember in school learning about how stars die.

My teacher explained: Many of the stars we see twinkling in the sky burned out eons ago. What we're seeing is ghostly glitter dust. Because everything changes, everything ends.

However, my teacher conveniently left out that this same stardust fate applies to us too, the fragile, finite beings sitting in those classroom chairs.

We humans are an odd species. We learn all about this inevitable "All Things Must Go Law of the Universe," yet we do everything we can to stick our heads in the sand when it comes to our own mortality. We're like, *Death? Never heard of it.*

We prefer to pretend like we're the outliers—the exceptions to the universal mortality rule. As if death is something we can find a way to dodge, like jury duty.

Our Mortality Denial game is both hilarious . . . and heartbreaking.

Because in the end, pretending that death applies to everything but us doesn't just set us up for a needed reality check. It also makes us miss the whole point of our impermanence.

The fact that we're all ticking entropy bombs isn't a bug in our life. It's an added feature. One that, if used correctly, can make our lives feel more beautiful and meaningful.

In fact, I believe that when you get cozy with the idea that you're on a countdown, you wind up cranking up the volume on living.

Imagine you're at a concert, and the band announces their final song. You're gonna soak in every note, every lyric, every beat, because you know this is it—no more encores.

That's what life feels like, once you embrace that it's finite.

You start to live sharper, love harder, and choose smarter. You upgrade your life to a higher, more premium level.

It's like discovering a secret spice that makes every moment of life more incredible. A pinch of mortality awareness can turn even the blandest day into a more delicious one.

Six Specific Ways That Your New, Unlikely Friendship with Your Impermanence Will Enrich Your Life

Motivator: Procrastination loses its grip when you realize that time is a non-renewable resource. That trip you wanted to take, the book you've dreamed of writing, the reconciliation you've put off . . . awareness of death whispers, *"Now is the time,"* urging you into action with a gentle nudge.

Clarifier: Suddenly, the noise of the world falls away. Your priorities become clearer. You know those grudges you've been nursing like they're going to hatch into golden eggs? Or that envy that's been eating you up? Death comes along, puts an arm around you, and gently reminds you to stop wasting precious time on this small stuff.

Deepener: Relationships gain depth and texture under the shadow of mortality. You listen more intently, hug more tightly, and speak more honestly.

Beautifier: Ordinary moments become extraordinary. Oh, the sweetness of a shared meal, a walk in the park, the ridiculousness of dogs wearing sweaters. Everything takes on a Technicolor vibrancy when you acknowledge that these moments are fleeting.

Self-revealer: Suddenly, the roles you play and the masks you wear feel like a waste of time. You start to act, speak, and love from your truest core self. You say yes to the unsaid. You kiss the person who makes your heart do the cha-cha. You become you-ier.

Liberator: The fear of failure begins to lose its sting. When you understand that your time is limited, the risk of not trying at all becomes far scarier than the possibility of failure. You become bolder, more willing to leap, because you realize that playing it safe is perhaps the greatest risk of all.

Here's the deal: You've got a finite amount of time, and it's ticking away. The universe has set the rules, and we've got to play the game. So I say we should learn to play it well.

Remember, death isn't the opposite of life. It's a part of it. It's the thing that adds value to every moment we have.

In the end, death is just life's way of telling you to stop dragging your feet. Make your days count. Make them meaningful.

This book will help you to do just that.

HECKLING THE GRIM REAPER: WHY IT HELPS TO LAUGH IN THE FACE OF DEATH

When you think about mortality, and the inevitable decline that comes with old age, the first thing that comes to mind probably isn't, "Ha-ha, good one!"

But here's the thing: I'm purposefully writing this book with a sprinkle of humor.

Why? Because let's face it, death is scary. And a little humor can make confronting this uncomfortable topic feel a bit easier—like sugarcoating a bitter pill.

Now, you're probably thinking, "Karen, I'm contemplating my own mortality here, and you want me to crack a smile?"

Well, yes. But please know:

My use of humor is not about making light of death itself.

It's about lightening the heaviness of the conversation.

In a way humor becomes like a softening agent, a way of kneading the hard, cold clay of death into something pliable and more welcoming. And so as I blend humor into this book, my mission is to make mortality more graspable, more touchable. Something you can turn over in your hands, look at from all sides, laugh about its odd shape, and then, perhaps, put in your pocket and carry home to study later, feeling a little less afraid of it.

Basically, humor makes the unbearable more bearable.

When you're able to laugh at something as daunting as death, wonderful things happen to your brain. It disrupts fear and anxiety... defusing their power over you.

It's like when you're a kid and there's a monster under your bed, so you name it something like Fred. And suddenly, it's just Fred, and not so scary anymore. **This is why humor is recommended with cancer patients.**

- According to a study in *Psycho-Oncology*, cancer patients who used humor to talk about their health challenges experienced improvements in their emotional well-being.
- Plus, the *American Journal of Lifestyle Medicine* reports that laughter not only decreases stress hormones, it improves immune function and pain tolerance—also helpful for cancer patients.

So if humor can help cancer patients who are staring at a close-up look at their mortality, imagine what it can do for the rest of us, who are mostly just dealing with the abstract idea of death.

Not only that . . . studies report that satirical humor doesn't just make us laugh. It makes us think.

A study in the journal *Psychology of Aesthetics, Creativity, and the Arts* reports that hearing satirical political material can lead to greater political awareness and understanding.

Humor's sneaky like that. It shows up in a clown costume—only to whip it off and reveal some profound, hard-hitting truths underneath.

Remember the role of the court jester? Historically, he was the only person who could mock the king without losing his head. But this jester wasn't just cracking jokes. He was speaking truths that no one else dared to utter.

Well, when we joke about death, we're the jesters to our own mortality. We're pointing out the absurdity of our fears and the urgency of pursuing our purpose—and thereby helping ourselves to more clearly see what's most important in life.

So my use of humor in this book isn't merely decorative. It's strategic.

It's my way to gently bring you face-to-face with the inevitability of death, without you running for the hills. And if laughter can make you stick around to think about your mortality, then I've cracked open a door that might otherwise have stayed sealed shut.

And I believe we need to talk about death more—so we can prepare for it and, ultimately, accept it. But the conversation doesn't have to be a downer. Instead it can be more like breaking the fourth wall in your life's sitcom. It can startle you into seeing your life's plot line from better angles. And you begin to recognize that, yes, we are all hurtling toward a final end . . . but oh, the spectacular views along the way.

Over time chatting about death can become yet another thing worth discussing . . . right up there with love, ambition, or the perfect way to cook an egg.

I believe it's crucial we talk more openly about death.

Because a life lived in fear of death is a life half lived. And you deserve to live fully. So I encourage you to laugh in the face of death. Plus laugh at the absurdities of life too. Laugh at the fact that no matter how much kale you eat, how many marathons you run, or how often you meditate, you're still going to die.

And that's okay. It's more than okay. It's completely human.

Which Brings Us to Your First Death Mindfulness Tool: A Journal

Why a journal? Because this book isn't just about reading. It's about doing. I'm going to throw ideas, questions, challenges, and prompts at you, and I want you to have a place to catch them all.

I've been journaling since I was a kid, and let me tell you, it's a bit like using a Ouija board—except instead of summoning ghosts, you're conjuring your subconscious. You sit down clueless about what's going to spill out, and before you know it, your pen is flying across the page, and you're thinking, "Oh, so *that's* what's been bothering me."

Journaling isn't just writing about what you know. It's discovering what you didn't know that you knew.

Since death can feel heavy, I want you to lighten things up a bit by giving your journal a funny name. Something that'll make you smile every time you open it.

For example, I've written on the front of some of my journals: "Selfies of My Soul."

Stuck for Journal Title Ideas? Try One of These

- Notes from a Future Dead Person
- Memento Mori . . . but First, Coffee

- Death: the Original Unsubscribe
- I'll Sleep When I'm Dead . . . but Let's Get Stuff Done First
- Trying Not to Be a Jerk Before I Die
- Death: It's Like Sleep, but Without the Snoring
- I Could Be Watching TV, but Instead I'm Writing About Death
- If You're Reading This, I'm Probably Dead. Kidding. Or Am I?
- Does This Journal Make My Mortality Look Fat?
- I Came, I Saw, I Wrote, I Died
- Welcome to My Pre-Death Diary: Spoiler, There's No Sequel
- This Journal Won't Make Me Immortal, but It'll Help Me Cope

Whatever title you pick, make sure it reflects the balance we're aiming for: honesty, humor, and a clear-eyed understanding that, yeah, death is inevitable. But thinking about death shouldn't suck the joy out of your life. It should do the opposite. Empower you to be a better joy seeker!

3

HOW TO BE GOOD IN DEATHBED

I've often wondered whether death was the universe's sassy way of dealing with human procrastination. After all, we humans are the best procrastinators.

Think about it. What if you had unlimited time? You'd probably put off everything.

- "Oh, I'll start my passion project . . . in a century or two."
- "I'll tell her I love her . . . maybe in a millennium."

Thankfully, mortality is here to tap you on the shoulder and whisper, "You ain't got forever, buddy."

When you perk up and embrace your mortality, you're forced to ask bigger-sized questions:

- What do I want to do with my limited time?
- What truly matters?

However, for the most part, we humans *ignore* any whispers from death, preferring to play make-believe with the finite nature of our lives.

As a result, we procrastinate on what truly matters. And our good intentions mysteriously vanish into that time warp called "someday."

This "procrastinatory thinking" is so common it's even got a fancy name: temporal discounting.

Temporal discounting is why:

- We say, "Someday I'll . . ." then never follow through.
- We choose immediate gratification over meaningful long-term goals.
- We waste an embarrassing amount of time on dumb stuff.

So, in this chapter I'm gonna help you to banish the word "someday" from your vocabulary by fully embracing mortality awareness.

Here's a quick reminder: We humans are the only species that knows we're going to die! No other animal gets the memo: "You will die someday."

At first glance, this might sound like a curse. But it's actually a gift. Because you can use your lucky human perk of "death awareness" as a built-in motivator to make the most of your time on this planet.

And to help you with this death acceptance process, I've invited a surprise celebrity guest to this chapter:

Aristotle, my favorite Greek philosopher.

I confess: I have a platonic crush on Aristotle. I love his philosophies so much that I even named my son "Ari" as a wink to him. Plus I credit many of Aristotle's philosophies for helping me to embrace my own mortality—thereby motivating me to live better.

For example, Aristotle believed:

You must begin all projects with the final ends in mind, from projects as small as bake sales . . . to that gigantic project called "Your Life."

He dubbed this concept "telos." Which is a scholarly way of saying, "Figure out your ultimate goal for a project, then aim yourself at this goal."

Aristotle put it like this: "Shall we not, like archers who have a mark to aim at, be more likely to hit upon what is right?"

Meaning? If you don't have a clear target to aim at, you're just shooting arrows into the wind.

And when it comes to the ultimate bull's-eye for your life? Aristotle thought the goal was the same for all of us.

Become your best possible self!

Yep, Aristotle believed we all share the same life mission, whether you're from Toledo or Timbuktu. We're all here to learn, grow, and become the best versions of ourselves.

HOW DO YOU ACCOMPLISH THIS MISSION?

According to Aristotle, you must regularly focus on the very *end* of your life—your deathbed scene. Envision yourself as the highest potential person you want to become, then hit rewind. Reverse-engineer it. What did you do to get there? Who were you to the people who mattered most? What habits, choices, and values shaped your life? Work backward and figure out what you need to be doing *right now* so you can end up as someone who's *good in deathbed*.

For Aristotle, the secret was simple: Choose strong core values and good habits that your soul can be proud of. Over and over again.

Aristotle also warned that most people mess this up.

Instead of aiming at the right target, they get distracted by shiny, ego-driven nonsense.

They decide their life mission is to . . .

- Become the richest, most successful person on the planet!
- Be the sexiest person alive!
- Achieve ultimate fame and power!

Unfortunately, if you choose these ego-directed, lower-level pursuits, then you will wind up with a rude awakening on your deathbed. You'll realize you chased the wrong rabbits—superficial, glittering, hollow goals that looked important from a distance, but left you feeling empty once you got them. You wasted your one wild, precious life on stuff that didn't matter.

And because of that, you didn't become your highest potential self. In fact, you might have missed the mark by a long shot.

If your *telos*—your ultimate goal—is money, fame, beauty, sex, or power, then you might wind up lying, cheating, and stepping on people to win those things at all costs. In the process, you'll sell your soul, ending up with what I jokingly call a *sould*—a sold soul—a brittle, knockoff version of you, held together with duct tape and regret.

The lesson? Aim your life at the right target: becoming the best possible version of you.

The problem? Most of us never stop to think about our future selves. We live for Now Us and forget there's a Future Us who's counting on us not to be idiots.

But as Yogi Berra wisely warned, "If you don't know where you're going, you might not get there."

By the way . . . there are many research-backed perks to focusing on your Future Self.

Here's a fascinating study called "Saving for the Future Self: Neural Measures of Future Self-Continuity Predict Temporal Discounting."

(Yeah, academics really love their long-winded titles, eh?)

Anyway . . . in this study, researchers showed participants a glimpse of their future selves using the digital wizardry of a face-aging app. They showed people what they'd look like several decades down the line. Wrinkles, age spots, the works!

Then, something remarkable happened.

People who confronted their future, aged selves were more likely to save for retirement rather than spend their money on immediate gratification.

It was as if coming face-to-face with their future faces ultimately slapped some sense into them. Like a cinematic moment, where "Old Them" traveled back in time and shook "Young Them" by the shoulders and yelled, "Wake up, you fool! Quit blowing all of our cash!"

The takeaway?

When you confront the reality of Future You, you think about your present choices differently. You become more motivated to improve your daily habits— to make Future You happier.

I'm explaining all of this for a very specific reason.

In the next chapter, I am going to ask you to do something that might sound a little weird: write your own eulogy.

Why? Well, writing your eulogy works for the same reasons as that face-aging app. Except writing a eulogy is like cranking up that face-aging app to eleven. Because you're not just meeting your older self. You're coming face-to-face with your *deathbed self*.

When you write your eulogy, you're forced to stop pretending Future You doesn't exist—and so you begin to ask some meaningful questions. What and who matters most to me? How can I live more true to myself? Where am I settling or veering off course? You'll quickly gain clarity on what you gotta do to make Future You proud.

Best of all . . . I've devised a way to shake off any creepy-crawlies and make this eulogy writing process playful, enjoyable, and simple.

I'm giving you a fill-in-the-blank eulogy template.

You just fill in the blanks, and *bam*! You've got a eulogy that doubles as a blueprint for the ideal life you want to live.

I've written my own eulogy, and it inspired me to make some empowering life changes. I've also given this template to private clients, and they too reaped tremendous benefits.

Why? Because writing your own eulogy is a powerful reality check. It forces you to break free from "someday purgatory"—and start living a life that won't piss off Future You.

Let's get going! Your Future You is waiting in the next chapter—and you don't want to keep yourself waiting.

4

EULOGIES: NOT JUST FOR
THE ALREADY DEAD ANYMORE

magine this: You're a ghost at your own funeral, invisibly floating around, eavesdropping on what people are saying about you.

Admit it, that sounds kinda cool, doesn't it?

But I digress . . .

My point: I want you to take a moment right now to think about your funeral. Then ask yourself the following:

- What are people saying about me?
- What kinds of memories and stories are they sharing?
- How did I leave a mark on their lives?
- Why are they shedding tears over my departure?

Got your answers? Next, ask yourself the following:

- Would I like to make sure the people in my life feel wonderful things about me because I lived a loving, meaningful life—a life with few regrets?

If the answer is yes, you've come to the right chapter, both in your life and in this book!

In just a bit I'll walk you through how to write your own eulogy. And in the process you'll create a vision of your ideal life, starring Highest Potential You!

If the thought of writing your eulogy feels daunting, don't worry. I'll gently guide you through the process. And you'll even have fun doing it.

Yes, I did just put the words "fun" and "eulogy" in the same paragraph! That's because I'm going to give you a eulogy template to make the process more approachable. All you'll need to do is plug in the words that resonate with you.

But if you don't feel comfortable writing anything, you can simply contemplate what you might put into your eulogy.

THE MISSION FOR THIS EULOGY EXERCISE:

To encourage you to take introspective time and ask yourself that age-old question: *What do I want to be when I grow up?*

However, instead of focusing on **what** you want to be **professionally**, you'll be refocusing more on **who** you want to be **personally**.

Remember: A eulogy is not a LinkedIn bio that's read aloud. It's a heartfelt account of the love you've given, the lives you've impacted, and the core values you've upheld.

The fact is, if you want to live a life you're truly proud of, you need to redefine success with a less materialistic focus! And this eulogy exercise is the perfect launching pad to begin making that shift.

Still hesitant? Think of this eulogy as your life's mission statement.
- It helps you to define your passions, purpose, and aspirations for a life well lived.
- It serves as a reminder of who you are at your core.
- And speaking of that word "core," your eulogy is also a *core value awakener*—reminding you which core values you most want to embrace.

Important Disclaimer:
Please do NOT panic if after you complete your eulogy it doesn't match who you are right now. You still have time to become "Aspirational Eulogy You."

In fact, that growth is the point of this book. After you complete your eulogy, the chapters ahead will guide you through simple, doable steps to bridge the gap between Current You and Aspirational Eulogy You.

For example:

Let's say Aspirational Eulogy You is remembered for doing charity work. Or for writing a novel. Or has an entirely different profession or family situation. Meanwhile, "Current You" isn't close to having *any* of those things.

No worries! In future chapters I will explain how to create small habits to bridge the gap so you can start living as the person your eulogy describes.

But I'm speeding ahead.

For now, just complete this chapter's eulogy template—and dream BIG.

How to Get the Most Out of This Eulogy Exercise

1. **Grab your journal.** This exercise isn't just about answering prompts. It's about digging deep. Use your journal to work through your thoughts before you fill out the template. When you're done, rewrite your completed aspirational eulogy in your journal, to keep a clean version handy for rereading often.

2. **Think in the third person.** Weird? Yes. But narrating your life as if you're not, well, *you* can help you view things more objectively.

3. **Tweak the template.** Change it reflect your strange, messy, one-of-a-kind life. Because nobody else is living your life but you.

Quick heads up: If you don't want to fill in this eulogy now, you don't have to. This isn't like one of those annoying "you must complete this level to unlock the rest of the game" book reading situations.

You can totally just read through the eulogy template, and simply think about what you'd write. The rest of this book will still make sense and be helpful, whether you fill in these blanks or not.

In summary: This exercise is optional. Like wearing pants while reading this book. Okay?

ENOUGH PREAMBLE. IF YOU'RE UP FOR THIS EXERCISE...
TIME TO FILL IN THOSE EULOGY BLANKS!

IN REMEMBRANCE OF OUR BELOVED [FIRST NAME]

We are here today to honor the life and legacy of [Full Name], a person whose [Top Core Value] and generous spirit touched countless lives.

In their role as a [A Key Role You Play in Your Life], they embodied the principles of [Core Value] and [Core Value] and [Core Value], using their unique talent for [Talent] to make a difference by doing [Impactful Actions].

They were not only known for their highly respected work as a [Professional Role] but also for being a person who showed dedication to [Something You're Dedicated To], and a relentless pursuit of [Passion].

In their personal life, their love was felt deeply by [Various Close Relationships], and the fulfilling times they shared together doing things like [Cherished Experiences]. These relationships were reflections of their capacity for empathic love and [Core Value].

Plus, [First Name]'s passion for [Passion] was not just a hobby, but another avenue through which they spread joy, love, and [Core Values]. For example, they [Memorable Story Related to Passion/Hobby].

A defining moment in their life was [Defining Moment of Overcoming], which showcased their [Specific Quality or Value].

[First Name] also hoped to inspire future generations through their vision for [Vision or Hope for Future Generations], encouraging others to embody values of [Values Important for Future Generations].

Throughout their life, [First Name] imparted important life lessons, including [Lessons Taught or Learned], which will continue to influence and guide us.

They lived by the quote [Favorite Quote], and thereby they were a living testament to the power of [Strongly Held Philosophy or Belief].

Although they are no longer with us in physical form, the ripple effects of [Full Name]'s thoughtfulness, [Talent, Skills, Impactful Actions, and/or Achievements], and [Core Values] will continue to inspire us all in years to come.

All done? How are you feeling?

Let's get real for a second. You just wrote your own future eulogy, which … let's face it … is kind of bizarre. Or maybe you just stared at the blanks, thinking about what you'd put there. Either way, that's still a win. You just spent time reflecting on the purpose and meaning of your life—something most people actively avoid, like taxes or group texts. So, good on you.

Okay. Now it's time to ask—what jumped out at you?

- Are you noticing ways in which you're falling short as a friend, partner, parent, or colleague?
- Is your pile of "someday" projects starting to look like the Leaning Tower of Regret?
- Are you realizing you're not standing up for what you believe in as much as you'd like?
- Or maybe you're itching to engage more deeply with a cause close to your heart?

If so, congratulations! That's the point of this eulogy exercise: self-discovery! Write down these reflections in your notebook.

The goal here is to shake you out of autopilot and push you out of your comfort zone—so you can live a life you're genuinely proud of.

Next step, notice which core values you cherished the most.

Grab your journal, review your eulogy, then make a list of your top core values.

Guess what? These top core values are going to be the quiet heroes in the narrative of "You at Your Best." They're the principles you will live by—the road map that will guide you from "I wish" to "I will." More on this … coming up soon.

USING YOUR EULOGY

Once your eulogy is complete, keep it handy. Revisit it often. Think of it as a handy gut check and reality slap.

(If you skipped writing your eulogy and merely thought about it, you'll want to return to this chapter to reflect, again and again. Reflection works best when it's repeated.)

Now, let's talk frequency.

You're not going to reread/reflect on your eulogy as often as you check your phone. That's overkill. But you also don't want to treat it like that gym membership you forgot about—until your credit card statement reminds you.

Think of your eulogy like a hit song on your life's playlist. You want to play it often enough to keep the tune in your head. But not so much that you start to hate it.

My suggestion: Aim for a bi-monthly review.

This twice-a-month check-in gives you time to actually make progress toward your goals, so each re-read feels like a loving check-in, not an annoying checkup. This isn't a nagging parent asking if you've done your homework. It's your Future Self dropping in with a high five or a kick in the ass, depending on what you need.

As you re-read your eulogy, engage with it. Tweak it. Delete parts. Add on new parts. Go ahead! It's your life, your words, your story. Your eulogy deserves your attention. The goal? Get excited about your life's mission—your *telos*—then become motivated to nail it.

THINK OF YOUR EULOGY AS A SUPERCHARGED VISION BOARD

Both your aspirational eulogy and a vision board give you a powerful boost of clarity and inspiration to accomplish your goals.

However, your eulogy is like a vision board on steroids—because it outperforms a vision board on many levels. Here's how:

Emotional superfuel. Neuroscientists Richard Davidson and Antonio Damasio discovered that our decisions are largely driven by our emotions. And let's face it, there's nothing more emotionally charged than a self-written eulogy.

Sorry, cut-out-picture-of-a-mansion-clipped-onto-a-vision-board, you're just not as compelling!

Clear targets and higher peaks. Psychologists Edwin Locke and Gary Latham found that adopting challenging goals winds up leading to superior performance. Your eulogy isn't a wishy-washy collage of Pinterest dreams. It's a detailed, ambitious map to your personal version of greatness that declares, "Here's what MY happiness looks like!" So, step aside, ambiguous vision board, there's a new sheriff in town!

A bridge across time. UCLA researcher Hal Hershfield's concept of "future self-continuity" reports that when you're closely connected to your Future Self, this leads you to make better long-term decisions. Your eulogy is a love letter from Current You to Future You. In comparison, a vision board's scribbled affirmations feel pretty flat.

Mental gymnastics for your psyche. Researcher Angie LeVan found that visualization can strengthen your muscles without physical movement. Similarly, rereading your eulogy is an immersive mental workout, strengthening your resolve and determination. A vision board might spark dreams. But your eulogy gets you in mental shape to chase them down.

What's next?
In the next chapter, you'll start transforming from Current You to Aspirational Eulogy You. And your bridge from here to there? A special tool that I call:

Your Daily To-Die List.
- NO, this is not a macabre wish list of people you want gone.
- YES, a To-Die List is very different than a bucket list.

A To-Die List isn't about ticking off adrenaline-fueled adventures, like skydiving, scaling Mount Everest, or kissing strangers in Paris. It's about embracing small, meaningful daily habits that help you slowly bloom into Aspirational Eulogy You.

In a way, your To-Die List is a "Do-What-Matters-Most List."

It's your guide to mindfully focus on what truly matters. So when you look back at your life from your deathbed, you'll see a path dotted with moments that helped you to live up to your aspirational eulogy. Join me in the next chapter and I'll show you what I mean.

5

LIVING THE EULOGY:
CONSTRUCTING YOUR TO-DIE LIST

Welcome back, fellow mortality mavens. We've spent some quality time crafting your eulogy. Now it's time to pivot. We're moving on to the next task: creating your "To-Die List," not to be mistaken for a mundane to-do list.

Don't get me wrong—I love a good to-do list. Mine is currently bursting with gems like "buy chunky peanut butter" and "clean out the mystery drawer in the kitchen." A to-do list serves its purpose, helping you to stay on top of your everyday life. But in the grand scope of existence, these tasks are footnotes.

No one at your funeral is going to stand up and say, "She was a legend at clearing her inbox," or, "Let's take a moment to remember her punctual dentist appointments."

Basically . . .

- A to-do list makes sure you pick up your dry cleaning.
- A To-Die List makes sure you pick up your core values.

So when your time comes, you can confidently say, "I lived a life I'm proud of!"

Think of your To-Die List as a collection of "bridge habits" that connect Current You to Aspirational Eulogy You.

Don't worry! This To-Die List process is far simpler than assembling an IKEA bookshelf. I literally know this as a fact because I've done both. And I'd choose writing a To-Die List over wrestling with an Allen wrench any day!

First things first . . .

Before we dive into your To-Die List, I'll share my own completed eulogy. Then I'll walk you through how I use it to build my daily To-Die List.

Karen's Aspirational Eulogy

Here's my eulogy, inspired by the template from chapter four (but tweaked and twisted to fit my own peculiar life).

Friends, family, and all those whose lives have been touched by Karen, we gather here today to remember and celebrate a life well lived. Today we honor her memory and the principles she stood for in her life.

Karen was a loving mother to her son Ari, a caring partner to Howard, a devoted daughter to her parents, and a supportive presence to all her family members and friends. To her closest circle, she was the person you could count on for a pep talk or a good laugh. To the rest of the world, she was NotSalmon, a bestselling author, philosopher, wellness enthusiast, branding aficionado, and mentor to many.

She believed in the power of curiosity, the necessity of courage, and the beauty of kindness. And she had a knack for making people feel seen, understood, and appreciated.

Her relationships, deeply rooted in empathy, deep conversation, support, adventure, and fun, were her ultimate treasures. Karen taught us that in the grand scheme of life, love is the bread and butter of a life well lived.

She was the architect of the profound concept of the "To-Die-For Life," a theory that transformed countless lives around the world. She lived her life in reverse, beginning with the end in mind, viewing the horizon with a discerning eye, choosing paths that led to meaningful, vibrant living.

Karen was not only a thinker but a doer. She walked her talk, embodying the principles she espoused. She valued authenticity, and was never one to shy away from hard truths, deep conversations, personal growth, and some feisty humor.

Okay, so the above is my eulogy.

I'll admit, when I first read the completed version, I felt a lot of ouches—because I spotted many gaps between who I am now and who "Aspirational Eulogy Karen" is!

But instead of wallowing in that discomfort, I used those ouches as fuel to create new, actionable habits—and they went straight onto my To-Die List.

WRITING YOUR TO-DIE LIST

Here's the daily process I use—and the one I want you to try. Crack open your notebook and follow these steps.

First, identify the gaps.

Purposefully look for those differences between your current life and your aspirational eulogy life. Where does today's version fall short of the ideal? This process of introspection might sting a bit, but hey, no pain, no gain.

Next, ask yourself this prompt:

Who do I need to become to get everything I want for my life?

Or, tailor it to a specific goal.

- "Who do I need to become to write that screenplay?"
- "Who do I need to become to spend more time doing volunteer work?"
- "Who do I need to become to run a marathon?"

Or use it to tackle a problem.

- "Who do I need to become to stop fighting with my partner?"
- "Who do I need to become to be the best mom I can be?"

The key is to keep the focus on "Who do I need to become?"

So grab your journal, formulate your question, and write it all down.

Next, answer the question you posed to yourself.

Brainstorm five to seven core values that, if adopted, could help you transform into Aspirational You.

Yes, your core values are going to become very important to you from this page forward.

As I hinted in the prior chapter, your core values are potent stuff. They're the unseen muscles that will empower you to become the person you aspire to be.

Why? Because who you believe you are—and what you value—will always influence what you choose to do.

Let me explain.

Frank Sinatra famously sang, "Do be do be do." Great tune. But as far as personal development goes? Totally backward. If you want to live your happiest life, you gotta flip it to: "*Be* do *be* do *be* do." Focus first on who you are *being* before you worry about what you are *doing*.

Here's why:

Right now, your eulogy likely inspired some amazing goals, like:

- Enjoy rewarding relationships
- Create a lasting legacy, like a novel or other creative work
- Give back through charity work

But here's the hard truth: it's all going to crash and burn if you possess negative qualities. You're unlikely to succeed if you're:

- Undisciplined and disorganized
- Coldhearted and indifferent
- Fearful, impatient, or self-loathing

Now, I'm not saying you're all those things. But let's face it. None of us are saints. We've all got a few "quirks" (read: flaws) we need to manage.

Here's the good news: You'll have a much better shot at living up to your aspirational eulogy if you embrace positive core valuess, like:

- Discipline and organization
- Warmth and empathy
- Courage, patience, and confidence

Meaning? You need to prioritize **BE**ing someone with lots of positive core values, in order to start **DO**ing those aspirational habits in your eulogy.

Your Identity Shapes Your Destiny

Who you think you are will influence what you wind up doing. For example:

- If you think, "I am a sloppy person," you act like a sloppy person.
- If you think, "I am a neat person," you will do things a neat person does.

The takeaway? You need to align your identity with positive core values if you want to develop better habits.

Now, it might feel like your bad habits are running the show, but in truth your identity is your puppet master. Your identity pulls the strings of your habits—not the other way around.

There's an entire area of psychology about this topic, known as "identity-based habits," which reports how your identity pulls the strings on your habits.

William B. Swann Jr., a respected social psychologist, coined the term "self-verification theory" to explain this phenomenon.

Swann found that we're hardwired to "prove" who we think we are through our actions.

- If you believe you're disciplined, you'll do disciplined things to back it up.
- If you think you're creative, you'll find yourself doing creative stuff to confirm it.

Your identity works like a self-fulfilling prophecy. Who you think you are determines what you choose to do.

Here's an interesting study that supports this:

The *Journal of Consumer Research* published a report in which researchers tried to encourage participants to vote. They divided the subjects of the study into two groups.

The first group was encouraged to think of themselves as voters, and to fall in love with the identity of being a voter.

The second group was simply encouraged to vote, and that's it.

Guess which group had a higher turnout? Yep, the first group. The people who identified with being a voter were far more likely to show up at the polls.

The lesson? If you want to kick-start better habits, start by developing a positive self-identity—*first and foremost.*

You gotta "**BE** do **BE** do **BE** do." (Sorry, Frank.)

Creating Identity-Based Habits

Here's the identity-based template I want you to use to write your To-Die List:

I am [core value] . . . and so I do [habit]."

This template works because it connects who you believe you are with your actions. And that core value/identity part? That's the magic that makes your habits stick.

Here's an example of how identity-based habits have helped me.

When I reread my aspirational eulogy, I noticed that I had described myself as a "wellness enthusiast." Meanwhile . . . Current Me was not exactly walking the wellness walk.

I still had what I euphemistically called my "pregnancy weight." However, in reality . . . pregnancy had nothing to do with this added poundage. Because my son Ari, at this time, was an ancient two years old! So, this "pregnancy weight" was actually my "I eat too much crappy food" weight—and linked to my torrid love affair with pizza and pretzel Goldfish.

I then had an honest conversation with myself via my journal.

What I discovered: I'm a huge fan of the core value "discerning."

- Professionally, I'm discerning—I care deeply about the quality of my books and online courses.
- Personally, I'm discerning—I put thought into the clothes I wear because I care about showing up at my best.
- But when it came to food? Total lack of discernment. Pizza and pretzel Goldfish were not the choices of someone who values discernment.

After writing about this in my journal, I decided to home in on this core value of "discerning" and use it to write my "identity-based habit," like this:

I am [discerning] and so I [eat foods that keep me at a healthy weight].

I started writing this identity-based statement in my journal every morning. Sure enough, it stuck.

I naturally became pickier about food—because discerning people make discerning food choices!

But that's not the end of this story about the power of identity-based habits . . .

Eventually, this "discerning" identity began to spill over into other areas of my life. Soon I noticed I was getting pickier about how I spent my time—and who I spent it with. I even started decluttering my home—tossing out old furniture and donating worn-out clothes.

It's really quite amazing how a simple identity shift can ripple through your entire life. And that's why I'm so excited to be sharing this system with you.

As it turns out, discernment isn't the only game-changer core value for me. Over the years, I've discovered seven core values that have been incredibly empowering in changing my life—and the lives of my clients too.

So, if right now you're staring at your journal with writer's block, wondering which core values you should focus on, hang tight. In the next chapter, I'll be sharing my core values cheat sheet. Plus, I'll toss in a few To-Die List examples from my clients too!

6

THE TO-DIE LIST IN ACTION:
LESS TALK, MORE LIVING

Let's get real: Most people don't think about their core values until something goes sideways. A breakup, a layoff, a crisis . . . *then* you start wondering, "Where'd I go wrong?"

Here's my advice: Don't wait for disaster to strike to figure it out.

To make things easier for you, I've pulled together seven recommended core values. If you pay attention to these now, you can save yourself a heap of regret later.

SEVEN CORE VALUES

These seven heavy-hitter core values will help you to juice up your joy and dial down those "what was I thinking?" moments.

1. Authenticity
2. Bravery
3. Curiosity
4. Discernment
5. Empathic love
6. Fun
7. Gratitude

Notice how they're conveniently listed in alphabetical order, from A to G. I did this so they're easy to remember.

I encourage you to remember each of these seven core values!

Why? Because these are regret-resistant sealants!

Let's dive into each one so you can better understand how they work their magic.

Authenticity

If you want to dodge regrets, you must live authentically. That means peeling off those unfulfilling layers of family guilt trips and societal expectations. You must own your quirks. Embrace your all-out weirdness. Step out into the world, not just as who you are . . . but as who you're meant to become.

Reminder: Discovering your true self is not about taking cute quizzes on the internet about which type of bread you are. It's about taking time for a little uncomfortable introspection. What lights you up? What pumps your heart full of joy? What do you believe in so fiercely that you'd shout it from the rooftops, even if the whole block was telling you to zip it? To be authentically you, you must put in the effort to know thyself.

Bravery

Bravery is non-negotiable if you want a life with fewer regrets. Not the sword-wielding, dragon-slaying kind of bravery. But the bravery to say, "I love you," "I'm sorry," "I need help," or "I disagree." Yes, it's terrifying to put yourself out there, speak your truth, or chase a dream. But if you want a regret-minimal life, you need to find the guts to do it anyway.

Curiosity

If you want to avoid regrets, you must regularly ask: "Why did this happen?" and "What if?" and "What can I learn from this?" and "What if I tried something new or different?" Otherwise, you'll keep repeating negative patterns—and never learn any lessons from your pain. Curiosity will encourage you to evolve. It will ensure that your stories are peppered with "and then I tried" instead of "and then I gave up."

Discernment

Discernment is your filter for for what matters most. It will give you the ability to say, "Nope!" to things that waste your time, energy, or sanity. It will make you a choosier choice chooser.

Empathic Love

Empathic love is the undercurrent of a truly meaningful connection. It gives you the ability to see beyond yourself and recognize that everyone carries their own battles. Empathy also empowers you to *listen more closely*—so you actually ask things like, *"Hey, you doing okay?"* And you stop fake-listening—like the *"uh-huh, yeah, sure"* stuff.

Fun

Yes, fun! Remember the thing you used to enjoy before your calendar turned into a tyrant? Fun plays a crucial role in keeping regrets at bay. It reminds you that life isn't just about chasing status and stacking up achievements. It's equally about laughing at silly movies, or breaking into impromptu dance parties. Fun isn't just a distraction—it's a lifeline. It makes the heavy parts of life feel lighter.

Gratitude

Gratitude is the ultimate regret repellent. It helps you to find joy, even in the toughest days. It's a lens that highlights what's good right now. So if you want fewer regrets, start hunting for things to be grateful about—with the same ferocity that you'd use to search for your lost phone.

Create Your Own Core Values List

I'm not saying these seven core values are the gospel truth for everyone. But they have proven to be pretty damn effective in my life—and in my clients' lives too.

But if these seven don't resonate with you, no worries. Here's a shopping list of **FIFTY** core values. Skim through and pick the ones that feel like *you*. Or at least, the *you* who you want to be.

• Accepting	• Calm	• Creative
• Accountable	• Compassionate	• Determined
• Adaptable	• Confident	• Disciplined
• Adventurous	• Connected	• Empathetic
• Ambitious	• Consistent	• Enthusiastic
• Balanced	• Cooperative	• Fair

- Faithful
- Flexible
- Forgiving
- Friendly
- Generous
- Growing
- Harmonious
- Honest
- Humble
- Inclusive
- Independent

- Integrity-Focused
- Joyful
- Kind
- Learning-Oriented
- Loyal
- Mindful
- Open-Minded
- Patient
- Persevering
- Positive
- Reliable

- Resilient
- Respectful
- Responsible
- Self-Compassionate
- Self-Respecting
- Simple
- Spontaneous
- Trustworthy
- Wise
- Zesty

Next, ask yourself:

- Which of my seven recommended core values and these fifty core values feel like they're part of my DNA?
- Which core values from my aspirational eulogy need to be on my list?
- Are there any other values I'd like to add?

Scribble down what comes to mind, then mull it all over.

Next up: Try a core value experiment.

Grab someone who knows all your weird quirks and epic fails, and who loves you enough not to sugarcoat things. Share your list of values and ask them . . .

- Which core values do you think describe me best?
- Which ones do you think I might need to work on?

You might be thrilled to hear they see you as "reliable." And slightly less thrilled when they suggest you bolster your "patience." Either way, it's going to spark a far more interesting conversation than debating what to have for dinner.

To keep things fair, flip the script!

Share what you think your loved one's top core values are—and the ones you feel could they could tweak a little. Sure, it might get awkward, but these are the kinds of meaningful conversations that'll bring you closer.

At this point, you should feel much clearer about which five to seven core values are most important to you. Write these down on a clean journal page. These will be your guiding principles—your personal compass.

Got your list? Great. Let's keep moving.

5-STEP TO-DIE LIST PROCESS

Step 1: Set aside five to ten minutes every morning to write your To-Die List. Think of this as time for future-proofing your life. I recommend mornings because they're like a reset button for your brain. Before the emails and chaos kick in, your morning gives you a window of clear focus to script out who you want to be.

Step 2: Write a "Who do I need to become" question at the top of an empty page. This prompt can be inspired by a gap you notice between Current You and Aspirational You. Or it could be inspired by a current life struggle or a goal that feels out of reach.

Example prompts:

- "Who do I need to become to get everything I want in my life?"
- "Who do I need to become to accomplish X, Y, or Z?"
- "Who do I need to become to stop doing X, Y, or Z?"

Step 3: Brainstorm core values that answer your "Who do you need to become" question.

Important: Try to rotate your core values daily, like working out different muscle groups at the gym. Today, it might be "discipline," which means you finally get around to doing that thing you've been avoiding. Tomorrow, it might be "creativity," and you find a fresh way to solve an old problem. This emotional cross-training strengthens all the qualities needed to be a well-rounded, mentally fit human.

Step 4: Choose one core value and one habit to plug into your "I am and so I do" formula.

For example, in the case of hunting for a more fulfilling job, you might write:

I am [confident] ... and so I [send out at least three personalized cover letters a day from 9 AM to 11 AM.]

Step 5: If you feel resistance to a core value because it feels too aspirational, try using this powerful identity-strengthening tool:

The old me used to [describe struggle with the new aspirational core value]. But the new me is now feeling [write the new aspirational core value].

For example, in the case of job hunting, you might write:

The old me used to [doubt myself]. The new me is [confident in who I am and what I have to offer].

To-Die List: Inspired By Eulogy

Here are client examples of the full To-Die List process, inspired by an aspirational eulogy:

John, IT professional in San Francisco

- **Aspirational Eulogy:** Known for his work-life balance and wellness.
- **Gap:** He spends most of his free time working or thinking about work.
- **Core Value:** Balanced.
- **Identity-Based Habit:** I am [balanced], and so I [spend thirty minutes each morning doing yoga or meditating before work].
- **Core-Value Strengthener:** The old me was [consumed by work]. The new me [embraces balance].

Angela, marketing executive in New York

- **Aspirational Eulogy:** Celebrated for her empathetic leadership and high team morale.
- **Gap:** She often snaps at team members during stressful moments.
- **Core Value:** Empathic.
- **Identity-Based Habit:** I am [empathic], and so I [hold a 15-minute Monday check-in to understand my team's challenges].

- **Core-Value Strengthener:** The old me [reacted quickly under stress]. The new me [listens and leads with empathy].

To-Die List: Inspired By Current Struggles

If you're choosing to write your To-Die List to resolve a current challenge, here's a new tip. Ask yourself this prompt:

How do I want to remember handling this challenge someday in the future?

Next, picture it—the way Aspirational You would move through the struggle, and the way you'd want to remember your story of triumph in the future.

Then take that vision of yourself—the you who showed up, who figured it out—and write it into your eulogy, as if you've already lived it. Like it's a story that's already yours. And think of your eulogy as an ongoing autobiography you're writing about your life.

Examples of the full process:

Ethan, a college student
- **Aspirational Goal:** Balance academics with being active in campus life.
- **Core Value:** Engaged.
- **Identity-Based Habit:** I am [engaged], and so I [spend one hour after dinner studying and another hour socializing].
- **Core-Value Strengthener:** The old me [coasted through college]. The new me is [fully engaged in academics and social life].
- **Motivational Question:** How do I want to remember handling this challenge in the future?
- **Answer:** I am immersed in the full college experience.
- **Eulogy Update:** At college, Ethan was known for both his good grades and good friendships—he was fully immersed in every aspect of his college experience.

Bella, a high school teacher
- **Aspirational Goal:** Inspire her students emotionally and academically.
- **Core Value:** Inspirational.

- **Identity-Based Habit:** I am [inspirational], and so I [start each class with a positive quote and a brief discussion on how it applies to life].
- **Core-Value Strengthener:** The old me [focused only on curriculum]. The new me [inspires students to live better lives].
- **Motivational Question:** How do I want to remember handling this challenge in the future?
- **Answer:** I am an inspirational force in the classroom.
- **Eulogy Update:** Bella was known for being a teacher who inspired her students beyond their books.

LOCK IT DOWN! HOW TO MAKE SURE YOUR TO-DIE LIST GETS DONE!

Writing your To-Die List isn't just about doodling vague intentions onto a napkin and hoping the universe takes the hint. It's about committing to the life you genuinely want.

Some of your "I am and so I do" statements will be more like mantras to marinate on. In those cases, slap these on Post-its or make them your phone's wallpaper—whatever it takes to get them stuck in your brain.

But most "I am and so I do" statements should be actionable habits for you to do—that need to be tied to specific times. And so you must schedule them!

The tough love truth:

If you don't schedule your To-Die List—and grab your time by the reins—something or someone else will. And your To-Die List won't get done!

You need to be bossy with your time. Without a defined schedule, you're like a ship without a rudder, drifting in a sea of endless possibilities. Sure, that sounds poetic . . . until you realize you're not actually going anywhere. When you align your calendar with your To-Die List, you take charge. You stop floating and start steering the course of your life.

Yes, there are apps for scheduling, because, of course, there are. However, I personally like to use my Google Calendar and a technique called "time boxing."

Um, Karen, What's Time Boxing?

Glad you asked. Time boxing is when you literally box out periods of time on your calendar for specific tasks. It's like saying to your tasks, "You've got from 9 AM to 10 AM to impress me! Go!"

In the case of your To-Die List, I want you to put those "I am and so I do" statements into those little time cages (aka calendar boxes)—and don't let them out . . . until they've done their time!

By the way, Bill Gates and other successful CEOs and visionaries all swear by time boxing. And if it works for people who build empires before breakfast, it's worth a shot.

For an extra motivational boost, I connect my Google Calendar to my Alexa.

Why? Because Alexa then nags me out loud about the task I have to do— making it even harder to ignore.

Sometimes I like to add a little humor to my "I am and so I do" statements, just to keep things interesting.

Here's an example:

I am disciplined and so I work on my *Your To-Die-For Life* manuscript every day from 6 AM to 8 AM. Because if I don't, Future Me will hate me.

At 6 a.m., Alexa cheerfully bosses me around with those exact words. BOOM—productivity ninja mode activated!

Here's another example:

If you're job-hunting, your time-boxed habit might look like this:

I am confident and so I send out at least three personalized cover letters each day from 9 AM to 11 AM. And I know in my heart that I am not just a candidate . . . I'm the freakin' answer to a company's prayers.

When you hear Alexa tell you those words, it will make you laugh and inspire you to feel just cocky enough to crush your job hunt.

As Johann Wolfgang von Goethe, that old German philosopher, once said, "Show me your Google Calendar, and I'll show you your future."

Okay, fine. He didn't say exactly that. Goethe actually said, "If I know how you spend your time, then I know what might become of you."

My point: Goethe believed your daily habits are like a crystal ball for who you're becoming. So, if you want to become *Aspirational Eulogy You*, then you've got to schedule your habits, so you actually do them. You can't just wing it.

But wait, there's more—we're just getting started!

In the next chapters, I'll give you an itinerary of practices to follow, starting from the moment your eyes pop open in the morning until you conk out at night.

I'll kick things off with an empowering morning routine. Because let's face it, the way you launch your day can set the tone for every hour that follows.

7

MORNING MINDFULNESS: WAKE UP AND SMELL THE CLARITY

In the stillness of the early morning—before you check your inbox, before you squish down your thoughts with Instagram posts—there's a suspended moment of pure potential available to you. A brief, untouched pause when the day seems almost hesitant to begin without your permission.

In these first few moments of being awake, before the blankets roll back and your feet touch the cold floor, you're given a minor but magnificent choice to ponder:

How will I live today?

You are still here. The earth has spun once more, and you with it. That might sound grand, but it isn't meant to be. It's just true. To open your eyes each day is to be given a gift so routine that it becomes invisible, like air.

But air is everything.

So here you are, graced with another day, with the opportunity for coffee, some conversation, and maybe even some laughter or discovery too.

But how often do you take time in the mornings to consider what all this means?

How often do you take time to ground yourself in the now—that is happening NOW—before the rest of the day tries to sweep you off your feet?

I used to think of the morning as something to rush through. My AM routine was a series of checkpoints. Shower, coffee, email. Check, check, check. It was efficient. But when I really thought about it, I realized that life isn't meant to be lived on autopilot.

Because autopilot doesn't take time to savor.

So I started to practice morning *mindfulness*, greeting the day not just with open eyes but an open heart and mind as well.

I'm not the first to embrace mindfulness in the morning. This practice is as old as Marcus Aurelius, that Roman dude who managed to be a philosopher and an emperor at the same time (talk about high-level multitasking).

Marcus famously said,

When you arise in the morning, think of what a privilege it is to be alive, to think, to enjoy, to love . . .

Marcus didn't mention "to drink coffee." But then, coffee didn't exist in his day. Which makes we wonder how our ancestors ever got anything done.

But I digress.

My big point—and it is an important one:

It's very empowering to start your day . . . by appreciating that you have a day to start.

Each sunrise can serve as a reminder to ask:
- What will I do with this new day?
- Will I live today—or will I merely exist?
- Will I bravely make today count—or simply count the hours till it's over?
- Will I let this day happen to me—or am I going to happen to the day?

Basically, you must take time in the morning to appreciate that you made it through to another day.

When you take that moment . . .you're essentially stamping your foot and declaring, "Here I am, and I matter." You're recognizing that with each sunrise you can craft a fresh, new narrative . . . and do some serious editing of yesterday's draft.

All of this brings me to a favorite mortality awareness ritual . . .

A MORNING DEATH MINDFULNESS PRACTICE

Now, as I mentioned earlier, I studied to be a yoga and meditation teacher, so I know my way around mindfulness. But the practices I'm about to lay out? These aren't your typical "find-your-zen-in-ten-breaths" routines. Nope. We're going deeper.

The mindfulness tools I'm peddling? They're not about zoning out. They're about zooming in—paying closer attention to the stuff that genuinely matters.

Practicing these death mindfulness tools is not just for yogis or for people who can touch their toes and pronounce "quinoa" correctly.

These death mindfulness tools are for everybody.

If you're thinking, *Ugh. More chores to add to my morning routine!* then think again.

These tools are quick, simple, and actually fun. Plus, you can do them while you're already going through your morning routine. And the best part? The more you practice these tools, the more you'll start aligning your day with the person you really want to be.

My morning death mindfulness exercises are sorta like brain-training exercises.

- You wouldn't expect to run a marathon without some warm-ups and training, right?
- Similarly, before a long day ahead, morning mindfulness exercises help you to tone up your brain with some mental conditioning, so you can manage the daily marathon of your mind.

Here's Some Research on the Perks of Mindfulness

A study from the University of Massachusetts found that a consistent mindfulness practice enhances both concentration and emotional regulation. Meaning? It's a bit like training your emotions to stay seated when all they really want to do is run around screaming.

Researchers at the University of California, Davis, discovered that regular mindfulness increases the density of your hippocampus. No, that's not a new type of exotic zoo animal. It's a part of your brain that's crucial for learning and memory. So not only are you calming the stormy seas of your emotions, you're also potentially boosting your brain's ability to remember things.

Another study from researchers at Carnegie Mellon University found that mindfulness training for only twenty-five minutes for three consecutive days reduced stress levels. I mean, if you can shed your stress in less time than it takes to watch an episode of *The Office*, why wouldn't you?

From Mind Overly Full to Mindful

Mindfulness—merged with a touch of mortality awareness—helps you to throw out the small stuff and zero in on what really matters. It's a reminder that "saving the good china for some far-off special day" is a scam. Newsflash: *Every* day can be a special occasion.

This morning death mindfulness practice will help you to tone up your mental resilience, so you can tackle whatever the day throws at you with the strength of a ninja and the poise of a ballerina. Or at least with less cursing.

The more regularly you use these exercises, the better your daily focus, patience, and emotional regulation will be. Plus, all of this brain training will come in especially handy if life decides to test your resolve (and it will). When this happens, you'll be better able to intentionally choose your response, rather than be bulldozed by your first reaction.

So step right up as I share eight different morning mindfulness exercises.

Now, I know what you're thinking. "Geez, Karen, I don't have time for eight of *anything* in the morning."

Okay, calm down. I know you're not a Tibetan monk. You've got bills, emails, and probably a toddler or spouse demanding cereal. And that's cool.

Here's the thing: You don't need to do all eight of these every day.

In fact, you shouldn't try. Instead, simply pick a couple tools that particularly vibe with you on that specific morning.

- Maybe one day, you'll feel like you really need to not hate the world, so you'll go for the shower mindfulness meditation.
- On another day, you might wake up feeling like your brain is a pinball machine . . . so that will be a good day for doing a sunlight mindfulness meditation.

Think of these tools as your personal mental gym. You wouldn't do the same workout every day unless you want one enormous right arm . . . and one scrawny left arm. Vary your routine to keep your brain guessing and growing.

And hey, maybe you'll find a couple tools that really work for you—like, they actually make you feel less like throwing your alarm clock across the room. If so, stick with those favorites! And please don't ever feel bad about skipping a few here and there.

The only *must do* among these eight exercises is the last one: Write your To-Die List.

So, without further ado, here are your . . .

EIGHT MORNING DEATH MINDFULNESS RITUALS

1. Bed Mindfulness Meditation

Before you launch from your bed, take a moment to pause. Spend a few minutes lying there, just being with your thoughts

Your thoughts are less guarded than usual, because first thing in the morning, your prefrontal cortex—that overbearing manager of your brain's executive corporate office—is still half asleep.

This means more access to your subconscious mind and less self-censorship. Your psyche can more freely wander your brain's back alleys—without that bossy cortex yanking it back to the main roads. So, it's good—beneficial, even— to stay in bed a bit longer and practice a mindfulness meditation.

Take time to note the texture of your sheets, the peculiar silence of your room, the slow dance of dust in the sunlight slicing through the blinds. Become aware of the ceiling's blank stare, the walls holding their breath as they wait for you to decide:

Who will I be today?

Let your thoughts drift around this question without corralling them too much. Listen to their strange dialogues, eavesdrop on them. Maybe your mind travels to last night's unfinished argument, a tender hope, a gnawing regret.

This is the most honest part of your day, filled with your most honest thoughts.

Don't direct these thoughts so much as observe them, the way you might watch birds skittering across the sky. Here, then gone.

The quiet of the morning will always have something interesting to tell you. Be curious and nonjudgmental about whatever comes up. If something whiny and negative surfaces, don't fight it, contemplate it. Get real with the "why" behind your "everything sucks." Shine a light on your patterns. Question your choices. Poke at your reasons.

Toss the metaphorical salad of your life. See what looks fresh and what needs to be thrown out. Then ask yourself what you need from this day—not what the day needs from you. Brainstorm one thing you're especially excited about.

Scribble mental notes. Maybe today you'll call your sister, start that book, forgive that hurt. This is your time—so make it less about what you must do and more about how you wish to be.

When you take that first step out of bed, do so as a bold declaration of intent. You are choosing to participate in this new day . . . regardless of yesterday's reviews.

Maybe even sit with your feet flat against the cold floor, feeling the shock of it, and think, "I am alive and thankful to be here." It's easy to forget that, to tumble from bed and into the day, the same way you've done a thousand mornings before.

2. Sunlight Mindfulness Meditation

Walk over to the window—and look. Really look. Observe the dance of leaves in the wind, the early birds going about their business.

All of this is a live-action reminder that life is always happening, constantly and beautifully, beyond your phone screen.

Look out that window and see what "looking" really looks like when it's not through a screen, not asking for likes or giving them. This mindful kind of looking is an old-fashioned noticing—and it should be an important part of your day.

When you take time to mindfully look this way, you notice how the sky is always repainting itself, never the same color, never quite the same clouds. It's a reminder that nothing, not even the sky, remains the same.

You too are like this. Every morning is your chance to be a little different, perhaps a little more daring. Consider this day your personal reboot.

Think about the sunlight before you—and the power of its light. It's not just filling your room but recalibrating you, reminding your body's internal clock that it's time to start anew. Science backs this up. Studies explain how the blue light spectrum found in daylight has an empowering effect on your body. It creates "melatonin suppression" and the activation of serotonin. And so this sunlight primes you for alertness and a better mood to face the day. Drench yourself in this sunlight.

If you can, take a moment to step outside and feel the actual light on your face. But if the day starts with just a window, then make that window count.

It's a small, quiet thing, looking out a window. But don't let its simplicity fool you. These moments are as potent as any meditation chant, as any yoga pose. They are your silent partnership with the day, an agreement to engage, to be present, to always keep looking.

So enjoy this moment basking in the sunlight. This is a moment that is totally yours, before the day becomes less yours.

When you move away from the window, carry the light with you. Let it perfume your hair and brighten your eyes. Appreciate that you get to have this new day, to stretch and grow who you are. Think of this new day as your do-over button.

3. Clarity and Confidence Training Meditation

Consider this tool to be your one-person pep rally, a way to kickstart your day with greater courage and a clearer head.

First up, set the stage with some energizing tunes. Cue up your favorite playlist—the one that gets your heart racing and your feet itching to move.

Try the Bee Gees' "Stayin' Alive" to remind you: "Congrats! You're alive!" Or play "Walking on Sunshine" or "Can't Stop the Feeling!" Or anything that makes you want to throw your hands in the air like you just don't care.

As the beat builds, let your body join in. Start dancing.

Yes, right there in your living room. Who cares what your cat or sleepy spouse think about your dancing? This dance is about letting go of inhibition and embracing the joy and silliness of life. Plus, dancing fires up your endorphins—your brain's feel-good warriors.

But why stop at dancing? Add some muscle to your morning. Throw in some strength-training moves—think squats, sit-ups, push-ups, maybe some weight training.

You'll not only build up your muscle endurance, you'll strengthen your mindset. After all, you'll know that you started your morning not just by rolling out of bed, but by rolling out a red carpet for yourself. So, you'll be ready to step into your day, with your head held high, fully prepared to take on those you-gotta-be-freaking-kidding-me challenges!

4. Mirror Mindfulness Meditation

When you head into the bathroom, don't just give yourself a quick glance in the mirror while brushing your teeth. Take time to really look at yourself, seeing past your untamed hair. There's more to you than your bed head, after all.

There's a soul there, a heart, a person who has battled life's storms and is still standing. There's strength in you that you perhaps you don't take enough time to acknowledge.

Acknowledge and honor your inner strength every morning when you look in that mirror. You deserve your own love. And not just as an afterthought. But as the first thought in the morning, each day. So start your day with a moment of self-appreciation, a nod of respect to all you've faced and risen above.

5. Shower Power Mindfulness Meditation

Multitask your morning shower as an opportunity to wash away not just the physical remnants of yesterday but the mental and emotional remnants too.

As you lather yourself up and rinse yourself off, imagine all your worries, doubts, and fears swirling down the drain. Goodbye, negativity. Hello, positive outlook.

Make your shower a physical and mental cleanse, leaving you ready to tackle the day with both a fresh body and mind.

6. Dress for the Life You Want Mindfulness Meditation

In the morning, when you stand in front of your closet, think of it as your portal. You're not just picking out clothes. You're deciding who you might be today, which version of yourself you'll be sending out into the world.

They say dress for the job you want. But really, why limit that to your job? Dress for the *life* you want, the *day* you want, the *feelings* you want. These are not just clothes you're choosing. They are mindset resetters and mood lifters.

- Maybe today you'll wear that purple dress, the one that says, "Today, I am creative, I am bold, I am the leader of whatever I encounter."
- Or perhaps it's the old jeans, the soft, frayed ones, because today needs to be a day of comfort, of self-kindness.
- Or maybe you grab the T-shirt emblazoned with a shark and the words "Bite me." Perfect for days when you need to feel mildly aggressive.

So perform this meditation by taking the time to mindfully dress for the life you want. You'll walk out the door feeling like you might just have cracked the code to the good-day algorithm.

7. Breakfast Mindfulness Meditations

It helps to start your days with a little humor, a dash of hope, and a lot of coffee. Because if you can laugh and caffeinate every morning, you're already ahead.

Personally, I'm always excited when it's time to head into the kitchen—because coffee isn't going to make itself . . . *unfortunately*. Trust me, if coffeepots could talk, mine would say, "Again? Didn't you just drink like a gallon from me yesterday?" Yes, yes I did. And I'll do it again today.

While the coffee brews, the eggs fry, or the oatmeal simmers, take a moment to be mindful.

Let the steam swirling from your coffee remind you of the dreams it's about to fuel. Inhale the aroma as a sensory cue to breathe in positivity and exhale any lingering doubts.

Imagine, if you will, the process of making coffee as an act of alchemy. Water, beans, heat—and presto—you've got gold. The same goes for your toast turning golden-brown, or your cereal reaching that perfect state of slightly soggy. These are small, magical transformations that happen every morning. Appreciate them.

Don't drink coffee? Try a smoothie blender meditation:

While blitzing those berries and spinach, focus on the whirl of the blender, the colors swirling together. Let it be a metaphorical reminder of how chaos can often lead to something good—even nourishing—for you.

Mindfully eat your breakfast.

Appreci-eat your food. Savor each bite. Recognize how everything you're eating is a miraculous convergence of elements (eggs, milk, cheese, butter), all of which had to travel a great distance through time and space to end up in your kitchen.

8. Write Your To-Die List and Schedule It

After trying one (or more) of the above mindfulness habits, you'll likely be in the right mindset to write your To-Die List for the day. Then—this part is crucial—schedule it!

Morning Scheduling Tip: I like to "eat the frog" every morning. No, this isn't some strange paleo diet. It's a productivity hack. The idea is simple: tackle your biggest, ugliest task first thing. Like, if you *had* to eat a frog every day (stay with me), why not get it over with right away? Once that slimy ordeal is out of the way, everything else on your to-do list feels like a piece of cake. Or at least, not like a frog.

Your Morning Mission, Should You Choose to Accept It

Make "death mindfulness" as essential to your morning as brushing your teeth—except it's for brushing your brain. Before your to-do list starts snapping its fingers at you, before your roles and responsibilities pull at you, take some quiet mindful time to just be with yourself.

Carve out a few moments for this soul spa time.

Yes, even if you're a non-morning person who considers Pop-Tarts and a black coffee to be a complete breakfast. Wake up a little earlier if you need to. But make sure you acknowledge the sheer improbability of being alive.

- Take the time to recognize that each new day is not a repeat—but a remix.
- Take the mundane—the steaming coffee mug, the buttered toast—and grant them the attention you usually reserve for the more magnificent.

After all, life is mostly made up of these small things, these tiny rituals that we perform on autopilot. By making these moments mindful, you do more than pass through the hours of your morning. You inhabit them. And so these acts of mindfulness are not delays—they're anchors. They help you show up and stay present in your life.

A daily death mindfulness practice ensures you live your life by design—not by default. It's how you can aim your day (and life) in the right direction.

Coming up next, we're going to talk about that tricky time known as "the rest of the day."

After all, it's easy to start your day bursting with the best of intentions. But then as the day goes on, your commitment to being your highest self starts to wane.

Not on my watch! Meet you in the next chapter.

8

THE MIDDAY INTEGRITY SLUMP: THE NUMBER ONE ENEMY OF A FULFILLING LIFE

So the other afternoon I'm getting ready to give a "You Gotta Clean Up Your Room" speech to my son Ari—whom I've dubbed my "Little Handsome." (My partner, by the way, holds the title of "Big Handsome".)

I launched into my usual spiel, "Buddy, it's time to clean your room..." fully expecting to be met with his usual theatrical groan.

Instead, my son hits me with this gem: "I'm sorry, Mom, I'm just not feeling it right now."

Honestly, I had to laugh.

I mean, how many times have I felt "I'm not feeling it right now"? It's like when my alarm goes off at 6 AM and I'm supposed to go to the gym, and I think, "I'm sorry, sneakers, I'm just not feeling it right now."

Then there's taxes, salads, and those courageous, difficult conversations with my Big Handsome ...

My son's cheeky quip got me thinking about all the things I'm tempted to avoid throughout my day—stuff I know is good for me, but that I try to dodge—because I'm just not feeling it.

The truth: These daily nuisances, these things we dread, they're actually kind of ... *important.*

Why? Because these seemingly small decisions we make throughout our day are quietly shaping our lives, influencing present events. They don't make it into the headlines, but they determine the plot. These daily mini-battles are more than chores. They're the unsung heroes of our personal growth ... *or lack thereof.*

More nuggets of truth:

The things we *least* feel like doing often hold the *most* potential for our long-term happiness and growth. And these opportunities are almost always preceded by a big, whiny: "But I'm just not feeling it right now!"

The reason we feel that resistance?

It's far more fun to seek immediate gratification than to delay gratification—even if we know there's an awesome longer-term benefit awaiting.

Examples of awesome longer-term benefits:

- Exercising my body = improved health and vitality.
- Cleaning up my home = a cozy living space where everything is easy to find.
- Doing my taxes = the assurance that my cozy home remains just that: *mine.*

Unfortunately, just because we recognize that hard work, patience, and willpower are important, that doesn't mean we embrace them. In fact, often when given the choice between chocolate versus salad—or sleeping late versus working out—we choose the thing that feels good in the moment.

And that's the problem. Day after day we choose what's easy instead of what's right. And that's how we wind up mightily disappointed by our lives.

I know about this personally. I've been lured in to take the easy, fast route on many occasions. I've over-eaten, over-spent, under-exercised, and blurted out things I regret. I've even gotten deeply involved in relationships far too soon.

Yep. Pretty much all of my problems (from trivial to tragic) have happened because I acted too quickly on my impulses.

Plus, our failure to delay gratification doesn't just trip us up in our personal lives. It ripples out into our world at large.

Look around ...

- Divorce rates are high—not because Cupid's got bad aim but because people often bail when things get hard instead of putting in the effort to mend what's broken.

- Heart disease is on the rise—not from bad luck, but from bad dietary choices.
- Credit card debt keeps skyrocketing—because we can't seem to keep our wallets closed.

And we all know that it's not always the smartest people who score the highest grades and draw the biggest salaries. It's the ones willing to delay gratification. The ones who put in the effort to study harder, practice longer, and keep showing up. That's how you climb the ladder to . . . well, higher ladders.

Here's the brutal truth: When you can't resist immediate gratification, you wreak havoc in your life.

The lesson:

Often the hardest thing and the most right thing are the *same exact thing*!

Every day you face the following choices, on repeat:

- Enjoy now . . . struggle more later?
- Struggle now . . . enjoy more later?

With this in mind, mastering the art of "I can wait" might just be the most important life skill you'll ever learn—*if you want to live a happy, fulfilling life!*

Not surprisingly, my favorite ancient Greek philosopher, Aristotle, was a huge fan of the core value of "self-control."

One of Aristotle's big beliefs:

One of the main reasons why people are so unhappy is that they confuse "pleasure" for "true happiness."

What's the difference? And what's this have to do with self-control? Let's discuss.

Pleasure (Which Aristotle Called "Hedonia")

Pleasure, aka hedonia, is all about immediate gratification. It's impulse-driven hedonism—hit-and-run joy—superficial and fleeting.

When you're caught up in hedonia you're:

- **Body focused.** Seeking lust, junk food, drugs, etc.
- **Ego focused.** Chasing superficial attention on social media, materialistic wealth, and shallow relationships that prop up your status but don't feed your soul.
- **Impulse focused.** Grabbing what's easy, quick, and shiny—ignoring your deeper self, core values, and long term growth.

Simply put, hedonia is the "enjoy now, struggle more later" package deal.

And let's be honest . . . that choice usually comes with a side of "what was I thinking" regrets. Basically, you're not picking true happiness—you're picking "eventual *un*happiness."

Which is why Aristotle pushed for a different path . . .

True Happiness (Which Aristotle Called "Eudaimonia")

Eudaimonia is "truer happiness." It's not about quick fixes or shallow wins. It's about long-term fulfillment. It's built on solid habits and deep relationships and rooted in core values that push you to reach your highest potential.

When you're living a eudaimonic life, you're prioritizing:

- **Soul-nurturing people:** true friends and love partners who understand you on a deep level and cheer you on to grow into your best self
- **Soul-nurturing habits:** activities and practices that are aligned with your unique self and long-term growth

When you're aimed at eudaimonia:

- You hit the books instead of the bars before a big test, because you value learning and growing.
- You practice a hobby you love, because it feels meaningful and fulfilling.
- You courageously speak up about difficult things, knowing a little discomfort now can lead to deeper, more lasting relationships.
- You talk things out kindly instead of waging a passive-aggressive text war, because you know that genuine connection beats temporary power plays.

When you choose eudaimonia life, you're signing up for the "struggle now, enjoy more later" plan.

Why is eudaimonia worth it? Because it leads to the education of your soul. And Aristotle believed that your soul is your ultimate G-spot for happiness.

Unfortunately, far too many people ignore their souls. Instead they go the hedonia route and prioritize pleasing their egos and bodies. They chase what feels good in the moment—bingeing on chocolate, impulse shopping, or swiping endlessly on their phones. They chase quick dopamine hits—that tickle their toes but never quite warm their hearts.

The cost? It's steep. They wind up with what I've nicknamed "soulds"—instead of souls—because they've sold their soul for that cheap thrill of immediate gratification!

What Do Hedonia Versus Eudaimonia and Souls Versus Soulds Have to Do with Mortality?

Quick recap: Back in chapter 3, we talked about Aristotle's belief that living your best life means you need to regularly focus on your life's end game: *how you want to feel on your deathbed.*

Aristotle's idea was simple:

The ultimate goal for the end of your life is to feel like you became the best version of yourself. That's the big prize.

To get there, you've got to reverse engineer your life choices—from that future deathbed moment to your current life now. Then, every day, you must make choices that your soul (not your ego, nor your impulses) can be proud of.

Let me tell you, your soul isn't craving the cheap thrill of hedonia. Nope, your soul wants eudaimonia.

- Hedonia is the fast food of happiness: quick, easy, momentarily satisfying . . . but it leaves you hungry for something more substantial.
- Eudaimonia, on the other hand, is like a gourmet meal for your soul.

It's rich, deeply satisfying, and nourishing in ways that stick with you long after the moment has passed.

If you want to be "good in deathbed," you've got to aim for that long-term fulfillment of eudaimonia . . . and avoid over-dosing on the fleeting highs of hedonia.

ESCAPING THE TRAP OF HEDONIA

In many ways, hedonia is a speed trap. You're cruising on autopilot, chasing whatever feels good in the moment, without slowing down to consider the longer-term costs.

Unfortunately, when you're in the middle of your day, with a million concerns distracting you, it's easy to speed right toward whatever instant gratification catches your eye.

No worries! I've got a little speed bump for you—a simple tool to help you resist those tempting "feel-good-now, regret-later" hedonia traps.

And when I say "little," I mean *really* little.

It's one of these guys right here:

>

Yes, I'm championing that tiny mathematical symbol you played around with in middle school.

In case it's been a while since then: This greater-than sign represents a comparison between two things. The wide part on the left means greater. The small pointed part means lesser. So, something on its left is greater than something else on its right.

Although I'm no math whiz, I like to borrow this symbol to create my own motivational formula, one that keeps me on track with my core values and steers me away from instant-gratification traps.

Here's How It Works

Let's say I'm at dinner with my family (Little Handsome, Big Handsome, and me).

We're about to dive into our meal, when suddenly my hand—as if under the control of some dark force—starts to reach for my iPhone.

There I am, about to disconnect from the two humans I love the most, all because I'm curious about what some random stranger just liked on my Instagram.

That's where my trusty greater-than sign kicks in.

It's like carrying around a pocket-sized therapist who's nudging you toward better choices.

I ask myself, "What's more important right now? What strangers on the internet think of me? Or actually connecting with my family?"

When I visualize this equation in my head, it's a no-brainer:

Time with my loved ones > Mindless scrolling

This isn't just a neat party trick. It's a core value resuscitator.

It snaps my focus back to what truly matters, steering me toward meaningful moments with my family (eudaimonia-level good times) over the quick, cheap thrill of an online nod (hedonia in a party hat).

The Beauty of the > Sign Is Its Simplicity

It cuts through the noise, demanding you to consider your core values in real time.

So, whenever the world wants to pull you into the trivial, I want you to visualize the greater-than sign and plug it into the situation.

Tempted to swap a hard conversation with your partner for some mind-numbing TV?

Reflective conversation > Reality TV

Debating between hitting the gym or hitting the snooze?

Feeling good all day > Feeling good for ten more minutes

Tempted to send a snarky email in response to a passive-aggressive someone?

Taking the high road > Momentary satisfaction

Debating between saying yes to a pushy person's request or guarding your time?

Self-care > People-pleasing

The beauty of the greater-than sign is it's always there when you need it. And so it comes in particularly handy when you're halfway through the day and your mind feels as busy as a bustling clown car.

Because let's face it: It's easy to forget your core values and aspirations when you're in the midst of a chaotic day.

Suddenly your To-Die List seems a million miles away, buried under the rubble of urgent (but often not very important) tasks.

Think of the > as a brake system for your impulses.

It helps you pause and refocus on your big-picture goals. Best of all, each time you use it, you're reinforcing your core values so they're more likely to stick around.

Soon, you'll notice a shift. You're not reacting as impulsively anymore, because you're not operating on autopilot.

Using the greater-than sign is like doing curls, but for your soul.

With every mindful comparison—*what matters more, this or that?*—you're beefing up the muscles of your character. And the more you keep choosing those "higher roads," the more you'll develop your "Up the High Road I Shall Go" muscles.

Yes, I love that pointy little triangular symbol. It sure knows how to get its teeny-tiny point across.

Need a visual reminder?

- Scribble a > on a sticky note and slap it where you'll see it. For example, I have this posted on my fridge: "health/energy > ice cream."
- Get techy with it. Make that greater-than sign your phone's wallpaper.
- Or set up a midday alert, a little > poke . . . for when your willpower's starting to lag.
- Or go manual. When you're facing down a temptation, form a > with your fingers (index and thumb). Hold it up to remind yourself what matters most. Consider this your new, less vulgar replacement for flipping off your bad habits.

Remember: You should never sacrifice what you want most in life in a swap for what you want now. A comfort zone might be nice place to hang out in—but nothing truly rewarding ever grows there.

Okay, at this point we've tackled how to manage your mornings and afternoons. But we're not done yet. There's one part of the day remaining . . . a time segment that can make or break everything.

In the next chapter, we're diving into your evenings. We'll dig into some nightly rituals that will help you end your day (and, eventually, your life) feeling accomplished and at peace. You'll learn how to clear the slate each night, so you wake up ready to inch closer to the life you're hoping to build.

9

NIGHTCAP RECAP: HOW TO END YOUR DAY AIMED IN THE RIGHT DIRECTION

Okay, people. Throughout this book we've been talking about the mother of all bedtimes. Death. The Big Sleep. Now, we're going to dive into why it actually makes sense to think about the Big Sleep before you go to sleep.

I know, I know. You're probably squirming and thinking, "Death at bedtime? Really, Karen? Isn't that subject a little heavy before sleep?"

But hear me out. There's a method to this madness.

Throughout the centuries, humans around the globe have created a variety of evening rituals, to be done right before hitting the hay, that nod at death's inevitability. It seems there's something about that tranquil twilight between day and night that gets people feeling all existential.

NIGHTTIME REFLECTIONS

Let's take a little trip through time, and across the globe, exploring some of these bedtime habits that might just make you rethink your nightly Netflix binge—plus give you a fresh perspective on that whole "dirt nap" thing.

Buddhist Mindfulness Meditation

Buddhists have a refreshingly straightforward relationship with death. They view it as the ultimate wake-up call and great equalizer. Death says, "You, with the spreadsheets and unspoken grudges—get over yourself. This ride ends for everyone." And Buddhists? They nod, thank death for the reminder, then get back to what matters. In the evenings, many Buddhists practice *maranasati*—mindfulness of death—as a way to release petty worries. Tibetan Buddhists take it up a notch with practices like Dream Yoga—where they visualize death before sleep to better appreciate life's impermanence. So, yeah—they even like to play 4D chess with mortality.

Stoic Journaling

The Stoics, particularly Marcus Aurelius (that emperor/philosopher hybrid we met in a prior chapter), had their own nighttime rituals. Marcus would end each day journaling about his actions and reminding himself that life is fleeting. His writings, now called *Meditations*, are basically Stoic TED Talks on how to live right. One of his key lines: "You could leave life right now. Let that determine what you do and say and think." Not your typical bedtime story, but hey, it kinda works.

Native American Traditions

Some Native American communities had a nightly mantra: "It's a good day to die." Hardcore, right? But it wasn't about wanting death. It was about living so fully that if it were their last day, they'd be cool with it. And if they did wake up, they were ready to crush another day.

Samurai Reflection

Premodern Japan's samurai didn't mess around with bedtime rituals either. Their motto? "Meditation on inevitable death should be performed daily." For them, accepting death was the key to living without fear. And when you're going into battle every day, you definitely don't want to be afraid of what comes next. The samurai were basically doing death therapy long before it was a thing.

Christian Prayer and Forgiveness

Christians have been practicing nighttime prayers for centuries, asking for a peaceful sleep and a peaceful death. It's like a spiritual insurance policy. A lot of Christian traditions also emphasize forgiving others before bed. They believe: "Don't let the sun go down on your anger." Because let's face it, grudges make for terrible sleep companions.

The Beauty of These Bedtime Mortality-Focused Rituals?

They're humanity's way of grappling with the undeniable truth that we're all circling the drain. But instead of turning bedtime into a sob fest, these traditions motivate you to live more appreciatively. They're essentially your bedside coach, reminding you that life is finite and so you need it enjoy it now, while you're still part of the crowd that gets to complain about Mondays.

Although these Big Sleep/Little Sleep practices have been around for eons, modern life has shoved them aside. Now, our nights end not with a gentle glide downward but with a crash landing. We numb the noise from this crash with whatever is closest at hand: the endless scroll through social media, the binge-watch of TV shows we won't remember next week, and then a collapse into bed without a moment of pause.

It's as if we're agreeing to let the day drift off without acknowledgment, like letting a friend leave a party without saying goodbye.

This autopilot mode doesn't just rob us of the opportunity to assess and appreciate our day. It steals our chance to steer our lives more consciously. And so we lose authorship of our lives, line by line.

So I want to encourage you to make one small change in your nightly routine.

This is a tweak subtle enough to manage—but significant enough that it will shift how you greet each morning. Soon you'll find that you wake up feeling a notch more at peace with where you are right now in your life.

NIGHTCAP RECAP: YOUR POST-TO-DIE LIST DEBRIEF

Instead of allowing your evenings to evaporate into a mist of digital distractions and mental clutter, I recommend you reclaim them by reviewing your To-Die List.

In the morning you took time to map out what matters most to you with this daily list. Next up, each evening, I want you to take out your list and check your day against it. Sorta like you're matching socks from a laundry heap.

- Did you pair your core values rightly with your habits?
- Or are you walking around with one blue sock and one pink sock?

By consistently ending your day with intentional reflection, you can:

- Spot your bad patterns and nip them in the bud.
- Notice your good patterns and reinforce them.

Your goal isn't to roast your day like an angry movie critic. It's to give yourself a fair and helpful review.

Could the protagonist (that's you) have made some better choices? Yes.

Were there redeeming moments too? Absolutely.

With this in mind, your nightly recap will involve a dual-lens approach. You're going to examine your day through two viewfinders.

The Stoic Lens

As mentioned, the Stoics liked to end their day with a metaphorical scroll through their actions. They'd reflect on their day's activities, then mindfully tweak their way to their highest potential selves. So I want you to use a nightly Stoic lens on your day.

The Oscar Lens

This lens is about embracing gratitude and celebrating your efforts—like Academy Award winners do in their Oscar speeches. When viewing your day through the Oscar lens, you intentionally highlight the positives of your life. Plus you reinforce your appreciation for all your wins—big and small—so you're inspired to keep doing them!

I want you to harmonize both these lenses.

- The Stoic lens will encourage you to pursue growth, resilience, and a focus on what's within your control.
- The Oscar lens will bring you well-deserved gratitude, joy, self-love, and a celebration of your life.

What does all this lens-looking look like?

Here's how to kick off your nightcap recap ritual, so you can feel like you've actually got some control over your life, instead of just flopping into bed exhausted every night.

Part 1: Pull Out Your Stoic's Magnifying Glass

Grab your journal. (And please, for the love of progress, don't tell me tell me it's collecting dust on your shelf or serving as a coaster somewhere.)

First, review the wins. Crack open your journal and start writing about the good stuff. What did you nail today? Where did you live up to your To-Die List? Maybe you finally told your boss what you think, but in a good, career-preserving way. Or perhaps you managed to not scream in traffic. Yes, small victories count. Write it all down.

Next, analyze the mess-ups. Now it's time to confront the not-so-great stuff. Why did that conversation go sideways? Why did binge-watching that series feel like a better choice than hitting the gym? Get it all down. This isn't self-torture. It's constructive self-critique. It's like doing detective work on your own life. You're figuring out the "why" behind the flop—so you can flip it.

Finally, set tomorrow's intentions. Based on today's journal autopsy, what's the game plan for tomorrow? Need to dial back the snark? Maybe actually use that gym membership? If so, brainstorm some concrete steps you should take tomorrow—for your To-Die List. This part is about looking forward, not just stewing in today's mistakes. Setting this kind of positive intention is like telling your future self, "Hey, I got you."

Remember: This practice is not about self-flagellation. It's about self-awareness.

You're doing this to recognize that you can't fix what you don't acknowledge. And that you will repeat what you don't take time to mend. With this perspective, you might want to end the Stoic review with some bedtime mantras.

Your Stoic's Bedtime Mantras

For Forgiveness: Hey, Self. I love you. You did the best you could today. Even if you didn't accomplish everything you wanted, tomorrow is another chance to make things better.

For Courage: Hey, Self. You showed a lot of bravery today. Every challenge was like a weight in the gym of life. You're getting stronger. Tonight, you recharge. Tomorrow, you conquer.

For Contentment: Hey, Self. Life's not perfect. It's not supposed to be. But you've got a patch of the universe that's all yours—and you're out there doing what you can to make the most of it. Focus on progress, not perfection. Okay?

Here are some quick tips on how to use these mantras:

1. **Say Them Aloud:** There's power in hearing your own voice. Stand in front of a mirror, look yourself in the eye, and speak your chosen mantra out loud. Think of it like making a verbal pact with yourself.

2. **Repeat Them:** Repetition is the mother of all learning. Whisper or speak your mantra slowly three times in a row. Each repetition is a step deeper into your subconscious.

3. **Write Them Down:** Grab your journal and write down the mantra as part of your nightly routine. Seeing the words on paper adds another layer of commitment.

4. **Reflect on Them:** After saying your mantra, take a moment to reflect on what these words truly mean for you.

Okay . . . time to move on . . .

Part 2: Switch to Your Oscar Lens

Grab your journal again, because it's showtime! And this isn't just any old journal reflection session. This is your nightly Oscar ceremony, where you're the star, the judge, and the audience. Get ready to hold up your imaginary awards!

The Oscar goes to . . .

You, acknowledging your wins! Scribble down those moments from today that tested your grit. Pat yourself on the back for the stairs you took instead of the elevator. Yeah, that's right, you chose health over convenience. Was there a traffic jam where you kept your cool? That's award-worthy patience right there. Did you remember to water your plants, or manage to save a tough conversation from going nuclear? Write that all down and thank yourself. Recognize the core values that you championed today.

Plus, don't forget to appreciate the supporting cast. Who made your day just a bit brighter? Was it a friend, a loved one, or maybe just a dog that let you pet it? Your journal is the perfect place to keep track of all the supporting characters that enrich your narrative.

Bonus Oscar Ritual

Have a fun time with your Oscar lens. When you brush your teeth, maybe hold your toothbrush as your award and give appreciation to your day. "I'd like to thank the friend who texted just to say hi."

Plus, here are three bedtime mantras for nightly gratitude.

Your Oscar-Winner's Bedtime Mantras

For Small Steps: Hey, Self. You ended the day a little better than you started it. Life is not just about big leaps. A lot of it is about these small steps forward. Rest tonight knowing you're moving in the right direction. Tomorrow, you continue the journey.

For Practicing Patience: Hey, Self. Today, you chose patience in a moment when you could have chosen anger. It's a silent victory but a victory nonetheless. Sleep knowing you're stronger than your impulses. Tomorrow is another day to prove it.

For Setting Boundaries: Hey, Self. You said "no" today when "yes" would have been easier. That's not just courage, that's, like . . . super courage. Tonight, rest easy. Tomorrow, you will wear your self-respect cape yet again.

Once again you can use these mantras in a range of ways: Say them aloud, write them down, reflect on them, etc.

Lastly, if there's something that feels like a big struggle, take some time to say a prayer to God or the Universe. Or pray in any way that feels true to whatever your belief system might be. For example:

Dear God or Universe, today felt like a battle with myself. I wrestled with doubt and insecurity, wondering if I'm on the right path. Please grant me the clarity to see my worth and show me which roads lead to better times ahead.

Hello, God or Universe: I'm feeling overwhelmed by the weight of my responsibilities. The pressure feels suffocating at times. Please lead me to the right people to lean on for support—and guide me to better circumstances, which will allow me to feel more hopeful and at ease.

Hi, God or Universe: I'm struggling to forgive someone who has hurt me deeply. Please help me to release the anger and resentment in my heart, replacing it with compassion and understanding, both for them and for myself.

Feel free to do as many or as few of all the suggestions above. Just do *something* mindful and positive, so you ditch the mindless nightly autopilot.

Blueprint for upgrading your nightly ritual:

- Trade your remote for a moment of reflection.
- Swap out the mindless scrolling for a mindful recap.
- Make your evenings less about passing out and more about passing on wisdom to your future self.

In short, transform your evening from time lost to time invested!

If you regularly practice these nightly rituals, they will help you to improve your life trajectory. Or, at the very least, they will give you better things to dream about than the cliffhanger from season three of *Binge Watch Island*.

10

TIME FOR A QUICK CIGARETTE BREAK

SMOKING KILLS.

You see this on every cigarette pack. The surgeon general's warning, a mini billboard that reminds you of your impending mortality.

Yet what do many people do?

Light up. Inhale. And with a shrug of their shoulders, decide, "Eh, I'll take my chances."

This is the equivalent of being handed a parachute with a warning label that says, "This parachute may not open." Then you jump out of the plane saying, "I feel lucky today."

Yep, that's us humans with cigarettes. Plus a range of other health warnings we're bombarded with, like . . .

- "Don't eat too much fried food."
- "Work stress is a silent killer."
- "A pint of cookie dough ice cream serves four."

We know these things to be true. Yet we often respond with a mix of defiance and rationalization:

- "But does eating a whole pint of ice cream count if I eat it straight from the container at 2 AM?"
- "Am I really eating alone if my dog is watching?"
- "If I walk to the fridge, that's technically going for a walk, right?"

Each of us denies death in our own quirky, self-destructive ways. What's your version of a death-denying metaphorical cigarette? Maybe:

- Bingeing on fast food instead of picking something green and leafy
- Scrolling through social media on every lunch break instead of getting a little fresh air
- Turning one drink into five because it's been "one of those weeks"
- Binge-watching TV until 3 AM and convincing yourself you'll catch up on sleep later
- Buying sunscreen but never actually using it because "it's just indirect sunlight"
- Letting your treadmill double as a very expensive clothes hanger

Each of these choices is built on the illusion of our immortality—death denial dressed up as optimism.

We like to think we're invincible, wheeling and dealing with our health and time as if we've got some secret stash of "extra lives" hidden away, like in a video game.

It's as if by dodging the truth, we think we can dodge the reaper too.

But eventually reality slaps you across the face. You start seeing the signs. Maybe it's a cough that doesn't quit. Or suddenly, walking up the stairs feels like you're scaling Mount Everest.

Yet we greet each death warning with a mental Teflon coating, so the omen slides right off us into the abyss of Things to Worry About Later.

- That cough? Surely, it's just a tickle.
- Those stairs? Well, they must have added a few extra steps since yesterday.

Then maybe something truly tragic happens, like the death of someone you love. Who smoked. Who got cancer.

Suddenly, the surgeon general is no longer just some annoying nag on the back of a pack. Instead he's now the Nostradamus of Nicotine.

And so those warnings about your mortality, that you've been flicking off your shoulders like annoying dust specks, now become a giant neon "Told you so!"

So why do we treat our mortality like spam email, acknowledging its presence with a weary sigh . . . before swiftly moving it to the trash?

Our talent for ignoring death is a curious tap dance. The answer lies in our beautifully complex, occasionally misguided human psyche . . . which is built to throw a wrench in our death-dar.

It's like when you see a wet paint sign, you know you're *not* supposed to touch it. But deep down, you really just want to—to see if it's truly wet. That's us with the concept of dying.

Death is the wet paint of life, and we're all pressing our fingers into it, just to see what happens.

WHY WE DENY OUR MORTALITY

Get ready. We're about to explore why we humans love to shove thoughts of our mortality to the back of our mental closet. We'll be unpacking the neuroscience of why our brains are wired to ignore the expiration date stamped on our backsides. And why we fuss over nonsense when we should be engaging with what genuinely matters.

Here Are Seven Reasons Why We're in Hardcore Denial About Death
1. Our Human Preference for Immediate Gratification

Blame hedonia, that primal pull toward "now, now, now." Our brains are wired to chase instant pleasure, even at the cost of long-term well-being. Why? Because evolution handed us this survival hack: prioritize what's right in front of you.

Back in the day, our ancestors didn't have the luxury of "later." If they didn't eat that juicy berry or dodge that saber-toothed tiger *right now*, there wasn't going to *be* a later.

Fast forward a few thousand years, and here we are, toddlers in adult bodies, reaching for the cookie jar even when we know it's going to spoil dinner—and maybe our future health.

2. The Cult of Individual Exceptionalism

Welcome to the ego's favorite pastime: believing you're the exception. This psychological phenomenon convinces you that while other so-called lesser beings might suffer the consequences of bad habits—smoking, binge-eating ice cream, or skipping doctor visits—you're somehow immune.

This isn't just ordinary denial. It's denial with a cape, soaring above the realm of statistics . . . into the sunlit skies of "it won't happen to me."

3. Cognitive Dissonance

This fancy term describes the process of trying to hold two conflicting ideas in your head at the same time. Cognitive dissonance is what happens when there's a clash between what you know (this tobacco could kill me) versus what you really want to do (light up another cigarette).

To resolve this mental clash, your brain pulls off some Olympic-level mental gymnastics.

You read a warning—"May lead to fatal lung disease"—and your brain goes, "*May lead?* Well, that sounds like a maybe. I like those odds."

Suddenly, you're betting your life on being the statistical unicorn who can smoke like a film noir detective and somehow outlive the kale-chomping marathoners.

4. Optimism Bias

With optimism bias, we cast ourselves as the invincible hero in the epic movie of our lives. And main characters don't get lung cancer. They don't even sneeze without looking cool. They laugh in the face of danger and flirt with disaster because, hey, bad stuff happens to other people, not to leading characters.

5. Confirmation Bias

This is your brain's version of selective hearing. It's the art of cherry-picking life stories that support our bad habits.

"My grandpa smoked until he was ninety-five," we boast, conveniently ignoring that grandpa was an anomaly, not the rule. (And that he actually wheezed his way through the final decade of his life—*in an oxygen tent*.)

Basically, we love collecting stories that support our bad habits.

6. Compartmentalization Skills

Compartmentalization is our preferred mental filing system, where we keep inconvenient truths in one drawer and pleasurable habits in another. For example:

Drawer # 1: "I want to live a long, healthy life."

Drawer # 2: "I live for the moment, and this moment smells like tobacco."

It all boils down to this: Every time we light up a cigarette (or do any unhealthy habit), it's a tiny rebellion against our own better judgment. It's like saying, "I acknowledge the future, but I'm not a huge fan of its work. I prefer the early stuff. Like now."

7. Terror Management Theory

Ah, the famed Terror Management Theory (TMT), the brainchild of cultural anthropologist Ernest Becker, then later expanded on by social psychologists Jeff Greenberg, Sheldon Solomon, and Tom Pyszczynski. This theory explains the mental acrobatics we humans do to avoid thinking about our mortality.

For instance, we panic over losing five social media followers, but don't spend much time worrying about our long-term health. Or we blow a small fortune on a flashy car instead of investing in a decent life insurance policy. Plus, we love to create a fortress of "busy-ness," hoping to block the view of the Grim Reaper lurking in the background.

TMT also explains why people chase after big, impressive goals like marathons or PhDs. These things don't make us immortal (sorry), but they let us believe we're leaving behind a legacy—a form of symbolic immortality.

So the next time you're scrubbing your kitchen's grout instead of writing your will, remember . . . it's not simply laziness. It's just your psyche playing an elaborate game of hide-and-seek with death. *Crafty, huh?*

USING DEATH AS A MOTIVATIONAL LIFE COACH

The unfortunate truth: It's tough to break through our hardwired human resistance to recognizing our mortality.

And so this is why the Stoics were big fans of repeating the mantra "memento mori." Which means: *"Remember, you must die."*

Cheery, right? It's about as jarring as waking up to find your phone didn't charge overnight. But I believe there's something to be said for this memento mori mantra. It's a profound invitation to really start living.

The truth is, facing our mortality doesn't come naturally. That's why the Stoics kept hammering it home with their memento mori.

But the Stoics were not the first to ponder the "death is inevitable" wake-up call.

Throughout history lots of cultures had their own way of saying, "Hey, nobody's getting out of here alive."

For instance . . .

In **Buddhism**, there's *maranasati*, a Pali term meaning "mindfulness of death." It's all about appreciating every fleeting moment, respecting impermanence, and not getting too attached to your stuff. To drive this point home, Buddhist monks created a practice that's as poetic as it is brutal: sand mandalas. They spend weeks painstakingly crafting intricate designs with tiny grains of colored sand, only to sweep it all away in seconds when they're done. It's the ultimate "accept impermanence" statement.

In **ancient Egypt**, they didn't just contemplate death. They threw it a grand party by celebrating death with majestic pyramids, elaborate tombs, pampered mummies, and a detailed *Book of the Dead*.

In **medieval Europe**, Christians slapped skulls, hourglasses, and wilting flowers all over their paintings like medieval Post-it notes reminding you, "Hey, time's running out, pal."

Folks in **Victorian England** took death reminders to . . . well, an uncomfortable level. They didn't just mourn their loved ones—they wore their hair. Yep, mourning jewelry was a thing: lockets, brooches, and rings featuring the hair of deceased family members. It's like saying, "You're gone, but now you're part of my outfit."

The **Japanese** have their *mono no aware* reminder, which translates to "the pathos of things." It's all about the bittersweet realization that life's beauty is in how fleeting it is. Case in point: the cherry blossoms, or *sakura*. For a few days each year, they bloom like nature's fireworks, and then poof—they're gone. It's the ultimate "enjoy this while it lasts" moment, which the Japanese love to weave into their art, literature, and mindset.

Mexico celebrates Día de los Muertos, the Day of the Dead, where they straight-up party with death. Families create altars and offer food, flowers, and mementos to their departed loved ones. It's like saying, "Hey death, you can't scare me if I invite you to the party."

So, while the Stoic philosophers have coined the phrase "memento mori," they're just part of a long line of cultures that believed thinking about death could really spice up life.

ALRIGHT, THAT WAS THEN, THIS IS NOW

Guess what? Modern researchers also report that when we embrace memento mori we get *mori* out of life. (Yeah, I went there.)

For example, let's talk about that rare breed of humans who have turned death into their day job.

I'm talking about your local mortician, hospice nurse, grief counselor, etc. . . . . These people live with a built-in memento mori—a constant reminder of mortality.

Weirdly enough, data shows these people are happier than most of us!

Take hospice workers, for example. A 2016 study in *Health Psychology* found that healthcare professionals who worked with terminal patients had lower death anxiety and a more positive attitude toward life (compared to their peers). Being up close and personal with death makes you grab onto life with both hands. These folks aren't wallowing in dread—they're out there marveling at life's fragility and soaking up its beauty.

It's not just them. Dr. John Troyer at the University of Bath studied death professionals and found that their daily brush with mortality gives them a heightened appreciation for life. They report having a sharper sense of what *actually* matters. They prioritize relationships over accolades. Experiences over stuff.

Even the University of North Carolina chimed in with a study exploring this "death-for-a-living" paradox. Their findings? People who work with death every day enjoy a healthier outlook on both life *and* death. They're acutely aware that the clock's ticking. But instead of spiraling into gloom, it lights a fire under them to appreciate the present.

Basically, when you're constantly reminded that life has an expiration date, you stop wasting time on pointless nonsense. You start focusing on things that actually matter.

This reminds me of a quote from the philosopher Seneca, who said, "He who learns how to die unlearns slavery." Meaning? When you face death head-on, it stops scaring the hell out of you ... and instead of being shackled to fear, you're pushed to savor every moment you've got.

The takeaway?

For people who work with death daily, it's not a curse. It's a catalyst. It helps them appreciate the fleeting beauty of life.

So maybe we need to learn some wisdom from these death-related professionals and practice some mindful memento mori—*so we too can live the heck out of every moment.*

Ready to Get In Touch with Your Version of Memento Mori?

Lucky you. Death is everywhere, just waiting to remind you that you're a temporary guest on this planet. Coming up, we'll explore a few death-related spaces that might help you reconnect with the fact that, yes, one day you'll be clocking out too.

Now, don't get me wrong. This isn't about making a morbid pilgrimage. Or ticking off some kind of macabre bucket list of Death's Greatest Hot Spots. Instead it's about considering activities, like lending a hand at a funeral, hospital, or hospice. Or simply spending time in deeper reflection whenever you make an unplanned visit to one of these places.

The idea is simple: Look mortality in the eye—and thereby add a little memento mori into your perspective.

Hospitals: These are like reality TV for your soul. You walk in annoyed about your Wi-Fi being down, and then, bam—there's someone battling with life-or-death stuff. It's a fast pass to perspective. You leave thinking, "Oh right, I'm not invincible. Maybe I don't need to lose it over that unanswered text."

Funerals: This is the original reality check. You show up thinking, "I don't know what to say," and leave thinking, "Wow, none of this day-to-day crap really matters, does it?"

Cemeteries: These aren't just for goth kids and ghost tours. They're like peaceful parks, but with a gentle memento mori nudge. You walk through, read some headstones, and realize we're all just on the conveyor belt of life. It's humbling.

Retirement homes: Want to know what really matters? Talk to someone who's seen it all. People in retirement homes are walking treasure maps of life wisdom. You'll hear stories, advice, and maybe even some wildly inappropriate humor (which, let's be honest, is the best kind). It'll remind you to cherish the now because, honestly, that's what it's all about.

So yeah, memento mori isn't about being a downer. It's about getting real with life . . . so you can enjoy it while you've got it. Because when you embrace the fact that we're all on a countdown, you realize: Every minute counts.

Remember, folks:

In the grand game of life, death isn't the opposing team. It's the ultimate reminder to play the hell out of the game while you still can.

Now, maybe you're thinking, "Okay, Karen, I get it. But how do I fit memento mori into my life? I'm a very busy person with dishes in the sink, deadlines, a new show to binge.

No worries! I've got some simple memento mori tools to slip into your jam-packed days.

For example, let's say you're losing it over some tiny inconvenience, like a molehill pretending to be a mountain. I want you to hit pause, then whip out an empowering *memento mori mantra*. Use it as a quick mental reset button—like this . . .

- Someone nabbed your parking spot at the grocery store? *Say, "Memento mori!"*
- Your coffee came out a bit too frothy? *Mumble, "Memento mori!"*
- Your internet lagged for a full two minutes? *Grumble, "Memento mori!"*
- Your favorite shirt faded a shade in the wash? *Whisper, "Memento mori!"*
- Your manager/boss/colleague/client was a bit terse? *Murmur, "Memento mori!"*

Basically, anytime life flings a molehill frustration at you, your response should be *memento mori!* It's your reminder to chill out, take a breath, and realize, *"Lucky me—I'm still alive. I get another shot at this!"* It's about seeing that little stuff for what it is: tiny, fleeting blips on your timeline.

Here's a bitter pill to swallow:

None of this day-to-day circus will matter when the curtain falls and you're on your deathbed.

Plus here's another, perhaps bitterer pill:

Much of what upsets you might not even matter NOW!

So, stop tripping over those molehills and recognize that much of what troubles you now won't matter at all when the end comes.

Here's How to Embrace the Full Memento Mori Mindset System

1. **Swap swearing for stoicism:** Angry? Annoyed? Miffed? Don't use your favorite curse words to express your upset. (Mine is "crap sandwich!") Instead of swearing, simply say, "Memento mori!" Or, if you're really stressed: "Memento mori, dammit!"

2. **Try a perspective prompt:** Ask yourself, "Will this matter on my deathbed?" This quick mental shift will be a great mood changer.

3. **Choose either action or acceptance:** When life serves you a crap sandwich (told you it's a favorite term), ask yourself, "Is there something constructive I can do about this?" If yes, focus on that. If no, focus your attention on something or someone that brings you joy.

And when it's especially hard to memento your mori, here's my personal five-step thought shifter:

1. If I feel myself starting to overthink, I pause and ask myself if I've thought this thought before. And if so . . . I ask myself if I've gleaned a lesson, insight, or solution from it.

2. If it's an old worry, I remind myself that I've already chewed the flavor out of it. So I need to refocus instead on something positive . . . or simply meditate/breathe.

3. If it's a new thought/worry, I focus on what aspect of the issue I can control, or what helpful insights or solutions I might find.

4. I remind myself: An hour of worry is even more exhausting than an hour at the gym, so I need to let the worry go!
5. Next, I either refocus on something proactive I can immediately do to change the situation, or I refocus on something I can immediately do to bring myself joy.

The Art of Discarding Temporary Troubles

Your mission: Become as picky with how you use your time as you are with choosing the perfect avocado. Become a time snob. Because just like that perfect avocado, once your time is gone—it's gone. You can't un-waste an hour any more than you can un-rot an avocado.

In the wise words of Ferris Bueller, "Life moves pretty fast. If you don't stop and look around once in a while, you could miss it." So, mindfully seize the now! Because who knows how many nows you've got left!

Coming up next, I'm going to share some death awareness tools straight from someone who knows a lot about life's final chapter and the regrets many people grapple with. So keep reading. Because in the end, the grand prize of life isn't avoiding death—but escaping your regrets.

11

LESS REGRET, MORE LIFE

I f you were to ask Death "What's one thing you're excellent at?" Death would probably lean in and whisper to you, "Highlighting regret."

You know those niggling thoughts about missed opportunities, unfulfilled dreams, and paths not taken? Well, they can all make appearances on your deathbed, if you don't proactively address them now.

George Pitagorsky, author of the wonderful book *The Peaceful Warrior's Path: Optimal Wellness through Self-Aware Living*, has spent time as a death doula. He's listened to people reflect back on their lives and has noticed a theme about their regrets. Most people regretted what they did NOT do, more than what they DID do. They regretted NOT living with more mindfulness, more courage, more purpose, more authenticity, more love, more balance, more joy.

People mourned the UNsaid words, the UNseized opportunities, the hands they did NOT reach out to hold, the leaps of faith they did NOT take.

As you know, one of the main themes of this book is about reverse-engineering your life—thinking about how you want to feel on your deathbed and working backward from there.

So right now we're going to look at these various regrets, and I'll share how you can proactively minimize them by mindfully embracing my seven favorite core values.

1. Authenticity
2. Bravery
3. Curiosity
4. Discernment
5. Empathic love

6. Fun
7. Gratitude

These seven core values are your regret-resistant sealants. When you slather your daily choices with them, you're basically putting a protective regret-resistant coat over your life, keeping regret from sinking in.

How do you apply these values, so you swap "I wish I hads" for "I'm glad I dids"?

I'm about to walk you through a simple process, so grab your journal and get ready to take notes.

An important reminder:

The goal is not to live an airbrushed, mistake-free life. That's an impossible feat—and perhaps even an undesirable one. After all, your mistakes are what make you achingly human and show that you are living daringly, bravely, boldly—which is always a good thing.

What you're aiming for instead:

You want to wake up and make some needed changes, so you don't let those big, soul-sucking regrets take root.

HOW TO AVOID JOINING THE "I WISH I HAD" CLUB

Regret 1: The Comfort Zone Prison

Most people build themselves a psychological fortress by age thirty. They set up the drawbridge, fill the moat with crocodiles of doubt, and tell themselves they're being sensible.

The thing about comfort zones is that they function exactly like prisons, except you are both the inmate and the warden. Nobody locked you inside. You just stopped trying the door to see if it would open.

You need to take risks if you want to die happy. People on their deathbeds rarely mention the great job they did avoiding embarrassment. They don't proudly recount all the adventures they decided against because something might go wrong. No. They speak of walls they built around themselves with their own two hands, safe decision by safe decision, until the walls were too high to see over.

To sidestep this regret, you need these two core values:

Bravery to step out of the comfortable and into the possible. And being brave doesn't mean you're not scared. It means you feel the fear but show up anyway, time after time, until being scared and showing up becomes your new normal.

Curiosity to ask, "What if?" instead of defaulting to "Better not." Being curious transforms fear from a stop sign into a newly detoured path.

Helpful "I am and so I do" statements for your To-Die List:

Statement: I am **brave,** and so once a month I mindfully do something that makes me uncomfortable.

Example: Every month I do one thing that makes my palms sweat—whether it's a dance class or a conversation I've been avoiding. I treat discomfort like a vitamin supplement for my character.

Statement: I am **brave,** and so I refuse to use age or time as an excuse.

Example: When I catch myself thinking "I'm too old to start" or "It's too late for me," I remind myself that I'll be even older next year whether I try or not. Then I begin.

Statement: I am **curious,** and so I practice "what if" thinking instead of "yes, but" thinking.

Example: When a new possibility appears, I deliberately generate three positive "what ifs" before allowing myself to consider objections. "What if it works? What if I enjoy it? What if this changes everything?"

Statement: I am **curious,** and so I approach failure as an anthropologist, not a victim.

Example: When something doesn't work out, I study what happened with genuine interest rather than shame. I collect data, not regrets.

Regret 2: The Purpose Void

Human beings are the only creatures on this planet concerned with finding meaning. Squirrels don't have existential crises about gathering nuts. Lions don't question their place in the food chain. Only humans ponder: "Is this all there is?"

When people approach the end, they often realize they've been playing an elaborate game of survival without ever questioning why they're playing at all.

They paid bills. They accumulated possessions. They watched television programs about other people doing interesting things. They regularly upgraded their phones. But somewhere along the way, they forgot to figure out what it was all for.

Basically, many people at the end of their lives suddenly realize that "staying busy" and "having purpose" are two completely different things.

Of course, having a purpose doesn't mean you'll save the world or become famous. Your purpose might be creating beautiful gardens that make neighbors smile. It might be raising children who feel deeply loved. Scale of reach doesn't matter. Meaning does.

To avoid this regret, you need these two essential core values:

Curiosity to ask the big questions before it's too late. Questions like: What makes me lose track of time? What would I do even if nobody paid me? What problems in the world make me angry enough to act? Curiosity keeps you from accepting the default settings of existence.

Discernment as the mental machete that cuts through the jungle of distractions, obligations, and societal expectations to reveal what actually matters to you. Discernment is what helps you say "no" to the merely important . . . so you can say "yes" to the truly essential.

Helpful "I am and so I do" statements for your To-Die List:

Statement: I am **curious**, and so I practice regular purpose audits.

Example: Every three months, I step back and ask myself: "Does my daily life reflect what matters most to me? Where am I spending time that doesn't align with my values? What am I not doing that I would regret not having tried?"

Statement: I am **curious**, and so I collect experiences that might reveal my purpose.

Example: When something catches my interest, whether it's beekeeping or constitutional law or watercolor painting, I don't just think "That's interesting" and move on. I take a class, read a book, talk to someone who does it. I treat potential passions like first dates—worth investigating even if they don't all lead to commitment.

Statement: I am **discerning**, and so I regularly practice subtraction.

Example: Every month, I identify one activity, commitment, or relationship that's taking up my time but not feeding my sense of purpose. And I eliminate it. I understand that purpose needs space to grow.

Statement: I am **discerning**, and so I pursue depth over breadth.

Example: When I find something that provides meaning (whether it's mentoring others, creating art, or solving problems in my community), I don't just dabble. I commit to mastery and sustained engagement, knowing that purpose usually emerges from depth.

Regret 3: The Workaholic's Lament

Next up in our regret hit parade: working your tush off and missing the best parts of life. It's the classic American tragedy—trading memories for money, moments for metrics, family dinners for "just one more email."

The truth is: It's embarrassingly easy to fall into the trap of overworking because our culture worships at the altar of The Hustle. We glorify the grind, fetishize the 80-hour workweek, and somehow decided that "exhausted" is a status symbol.

I confess I was a sucker for Beast Mode. I even had a sticker on my bathroom mirror with those exact words, to motivate myself. Unfortunately living in Beast Mode felt like I was a smartphone on 1 percent battery . . . all the freaking time.

Thankfully, one day it clicked: all that busyness didn't actually make me a more valuable human. It just made me tired and cranky. Yet there I was, thinking if I worked harder, faster, and did more every day, I'd somehow be . . . I don't know, a superhero? Spoiler: I wasn't. So I switched to what I now call Best Mode.

Here's the difference.

Beast Mode: I'd wake up, chug two coffees, and skip breakfast because "I didn't have time." I'd sprint through emails, juggle a million tasks, maybe remember to eat lunch around 3 pm. By 9pm I'd collapse on the couch, thinking, "Look at me, I did everything." But I wasn't happy. I was a zombie running on fumes.

Best Mode: I now start my day with mindfulness exercises, actually eat breakfast, and focus on a just few key priorities. I pace myself. I take breaks, drink water (not just coffee), and remember that there's a life outside my inbox.

By the end of the day, I'm a happy person who got things done and enjoyed life along the way.

The quickie difference Beast Mode vs. Best Mode?

Beast Mode is all go, go, go—with maximum effort, maximum speed, maximum output. It works in the short-term, but often leads to burnout and losing sight of what matters.

Best Mode is about sustainability, balance, and intention. It prioritizes self-care, reflection, mindful action—and living your best life, not just the busiest.

The clunky elephant in the room:

The grim reality is that for many people Beast Mode isn't a choice. It's survival mode. You're hustling non-stop just to keep food on the table and the lights on. If that's where you're at, I get it. But even in survival mode, it's crucial to carve out something—a moment to laugh, love, or just breathe. Life isn't only about surviving. It's about living.

For protection against this regret, you'll need to embrace these two core values:

Discernment will be your BS detector, helping you distinguish between what's truly important and what's just urgent-looking noise. It's the skill of knowing when to say "hell yes" and when to say "not a chance."

Fun will be your reminder that you're a human being, not a human doing. It keeps you from turning into a sad, joyless productivity machine with great KPIs but zero joy.

Helpful "I am and so I do" statements for your To-Die List:

Statement: I am **discerning**, and so I treat my time like it's a VIP backstage pass—not everyone gets access.

Example: I set fierce boundaries around my calendar, saying no to meetings that could be emails, projects that don't align with my values, and energy vampires who want to suck my time dry.

Statement: I am **discerning**, so I regularly audit my commitments like I'm the IRS and they're suspicious tax returns.

Example: Once a month, I get brutally honest about how I'm spending my days. I ask myself: "If I were on my deathbed looking back, would I be glad I spent 20 hours a week on this?" If the answer is a hard no, I find a way to delegate, delete, or dramatically reduce that commitment.

Statement: I am **fun**, so I declare "fun emergencies" with the same urgency I'd give actual emergencies.

Example: When I notice I haven't laughed in days or can't remember my last non-work-related conversation, I drop everything for an impromptu fun break—whether that's a midday movie, an unplanned road trip, or just dancing wildly in my kitchen to '90s hip-hop.

Statement: I am **fun,** and so I keep a "fun jar" filled with quick, joyful break ideas.

Example: Whenever I think of a fun activity, I write it down and drop it in the jar—like trying a new escape room, podcast, dance class, home-cooked recipe, or hiking trail. If I need a pick-me-up, I pull out an idea, and just do it. It's like keeping an emergency stash of happiness.

Regret 4: The Authenticity Bypass

Far too many of us contort ourselves into human pretzels trying to please Mom, impress Dad, fit in with the cool kids, and check all those socially-approved boxes. You know the drill: go to this school, marry this type, buy a house in this neighborhood, pursue this career, post these photos. It's like we're all wearing these itchy, constricting costumes for the applause of an audience that, let's face it, is mostly checking their phones anyway.

If you want to dodge this particular regret bullet, you need these two core values:

Bravery, to finally rip off that itchy costume and declare: "This is me—deal with it." It's about standing in your own weird light even when everyone's shouting for you to step back into the shadows.

Authenticity, to recognize deep in your bones that "approval from others" is a crappy substitute for self-acceptance.

Helpful "I am and so I do" statements for your To-Die List:

Statement: I am **authentic,** and so I practice "authenticity pauses."

Example: When faced with a decision, I reflect on whether my choice aligns with my truest self before I spend time doing something.

Statement: I am **authentic,** and so I pursue hobbies and interests that intrigue me, not what's trendy or expected.

Example: Before I jump into a new project or RSVP to an event, I take a beat to figure out if it's really my jam . . . or if I'm just trying to fit in, please others or do what's popular.

Statement: I am **brave**, and so I initiate difficult conversations that are necessary for growth and resolution.

Example: I tackle issues head-on in my personal and professional relationships . . . instead of avoiding conflict.

Statement: I am **brave**, and so I take risks to pursue what truly fulfills me, even if there's a chance of failure.

Example: I apply for that dream job or start that business I've always thought about . . . despite the fear of rejection or failure.

Regret 5: The Truth-Telling Deficit

We have hundreds of thousands of words in the English language, yet most people rely on "fine" to describe everything from mild contentment to soul-crushing despair.

As a result, many people on their death beds wind up regretting that their inside voice didn't match their outside voice. Their thoughts said, "I'm hurt," while their mouths said, "No problem." Their hearts screamed, "I need help," while their emails read, "I've got this handled." Their souls whispered, "I love you," while their lips muttered, "See you around."

The accumulated distance between what we think and what we say makes meaningful connection far harder.

The truth is: most people avoid straight talk for perfectly understandable reasons. They don't want to rock the boat. They fear rejection. They worry that honest expression might cost them relationships, promotions, or holiday dinner invitations. So they translate their raw feelings through a politeness filter so effective it strips away all meaning. "I'm furious" becomes "I'm a little concerned." "I'm devastated" transforms into "That's disappointing." "I need you" morphs into "Whatever works for your schedule."

The price of this constant translation isn't just miscommunication. It's a feeling of loneliness, of not being seen, heard, understood.

To avoid this regret, you need these two core values:

Curiosity, to understand what limiting beliefs are blocking you from speaking your truth. Fear of rejection? Fear of being seen as weak? Who did you learn this from? Plus, you need to become curious about what awesome things might happen if you start to express yourself more.

Bravery is what gets you to open your mouth and say what needs to be said. Reminder: Bravery isn't about lack of fear. It's about choosing to talk louder than your insecurities.

Helpful "I am and so I do" statements for your To-Die List:

Statement: I am **curious,** and so I play devil's advocate with myself.

Example: For every feeling I suppress, I argue both sides in my journal. Why should I say it? Why shouldn't I? This mental tug-of-war helps clarify if my silence is protecting me or holding me back.

Statement: I am **curious,** and so I seek out emotional mentors.

Example: I find people who are great at expressing themselves—a friend, therapist, or role model. I ask them directly why they think I'm not expressing myself and stay open-minded to what they say.

Statement: I am **brave,** and so I step out of my comfort zone and share more vulnerable moments with loved ones.

Example: In safe settings, I share something personal—normalizing vulnerability as strength, not weakness.

Statement: I am **brave,** and so I use "I feel" statements in tough conversations.

Example: I anchor difficult discussions with "I feel" statements, to own my emotional truth without casting blame—thereby making it easier for others to hear me without becoming defensive.

Regret 6: Procrastinating Joy

This one hurts. People get to the end of their lives and realize, "Oh, crap—I could've just chosen to enjoy myself more." Unfortunately many people realize too late that they had allowed worry, fear, and societal expectations to cloud the simple joys of life.

A big troublemaker behind this regret: We're all sold a lie that happiness is located somewhere out there—in a bigger house, a better job, a more perfect relationship. We're led to believe that happiness is always one promotion, one lottery win, or one crash diet away.

When happiness is always a future destination, you're basically on a treadmill chasing a carrot you'll never eat. Spoiler: You're the donkey in this metaphor.

Here's the truth: Happiness is here right now, all around you—it's just buried under all the crap you've convinced yourself matters more. It's in small moments: the joy of a perfectly toasted bagel, a laugh that makes you snort, or nailing the perfect parallel park on the first try.

If you want to dodge this sixth regret, you need to embrace these two core values:

Fun keeps you from turning into a sad, joyless productivity machine. Stop treating fun like an afterthought. Make time to watch a dumb movie, jump in the ocean, and reconnect with the playfulness of life.

Gratitude is an antidote to regret—because it helps you to focus on what you have, not what you've lost or never achieved. Gratitude makes it easier to avoid the trap of always chasing more.

Helpful "I am and so I do" statements for your To-Die List:

Statement: I am **fun,** and so I start work meetings with a two-minute dance party.

Example: It doesn't matter if it's a Zoom call or an in-person meeting, I blast a song, and everyone gets two minutes to dance off the stress. Yes, it's ridiculous, but it loosens people up, and makes even the Monday-est Mondays better.

Statement: I am **fun,** and so I maintain a "ridiculous goals" list.

Example: I keep a running list of slightly absurd achievements I want to accomplish—learning to juggle, mastering a magic trick, perfecting a celebrity impression, or baking the world's most complicated cookie recipe. These goals have no practical value except bringing joy, which makes them especially valuable.

Statement: I am **grateful,** and so I keep a gratitude sketchbook.

Example: Instead of writing down what I'm thankful for, I sketch it. A great meal, a friend's smile, a sunny day. It's a visual scrapbook of life's blessings.

Statement: I am **grateful,** and so I turn negatives into positives, complaints into compliments.

Example: If I catch myself complaining about something, I flip it into a compliment or find a reason to be thankful. Whining about the rain? I appreciate how it nourishes the garden. Stuck in traffic? I think about how I'm lucky

Less Regret, More Life   91

to have a car, and that it's taking me home to my favorite people and my comfy couch.

LET'S WRAP THIS BABY UP

There you have it, a regret reversal system—your cheat codes to level up your life and dial down on future remorse.

Next up . . . we're going to look at what the people who've already exited stage left can teach us about living better now.

In the next chapter, I'm gonna get personal and share what losing my dad taught me about life.

Meet you on the next page . . .

12

LEAVING RIPPLES: HOW THE DEATH OF A LOVED ONE TEACHES US TO LIVE

On the day my father passed away (a few decades ago), a strange and beautiful synchronicity happened.

My mom discovered an envelope tucked away in a corner of my dad's bureau drawer. It was something I'd mailed to my dad way back in the 1980s, during my college years.

Inside the envelope were several pages I'd ripped from a book—whose title I no longer remembered. Instantly I became curious to read what my dad had found so important that he had actually saved it for a few decades.

As luck—or fate, or whatever trickster pulls the cosmic strings—would have it, the words on the page were about how to survive the grief of a lost loved one.

The timing was eerie, unsettling even. But there these words were, talking to me about how to wade through the sadness of my loss and navigate the start of my life without my dad.

I found this book's clipping so poignant that I read it as my dad's eulogy.

Even though the actual clipping itself has since been lost, I still remember what it said.

Here's the gist.

It began with a poignant reminder: "Everything that is not given, is lost."

The pages then explained that every thought and feeling you have, every beautiful moment you experience, every talent you're gifted—all of it is meaningless unless you share it with others.

By giving freely of your mind, heart, and spirit, you ensure that what matters most to you doesn't die with you. Instead, it lives on in the people you touch, and in the people they touch, and so on.

It's like tossing a pebble into a pond. Each gift you share creates ripples that radiate outward, reaching places you'll never see.

But if you hold back, if you keep your heart and essence locked away, your ripples will be small and short-lived.

Viewed this way . . . you should take time to think about what kind of ripple you want to leave behind.

Wow. That metaphor about the tiny pebble and its big ripples hit me hard. And reading about all this on the day that my dad died made me reflect on the ripples he left behind . . . *radiating outward to me.*

I thought about his kindness. His quirky humor. And his reputation as a contrarian thinker in his career as a stockbroker.

For example, I remembered how once when everyone was freaking out during a market crash, my dad was surprisingly unfazed. He told me why. "The market crash isn't entirely bad," he said. "It just means everything's temporarily on sale!"

Yep, my dad was not one to follow the crowd.

A few months after his death, when I was thinking back on my dad, I had an epiphany. Although I didn't have a career in finance (like him), I had still inherited his core value of "contrarian thinking." And I had applied this quality to my career in writing, in the form of my defiant approach to books.

For example, when I pitched my book *How To Be Happy, Dammit* to my agent, she tried desperately to talk me out of it. She insisted nobody wanted a feisty-titled self-help book. It went against the market norms. But because I inherited my dad's contrarian spirit, I trusted my instincts and pushed forward nonetheless. Sure enough, that book became a huge bestseller and a breakthrough for my career.

As it turned out, the apple (or pebble?) didn't fall far from the tree.

CREATING RIPPLES

After my dad passed, I decided to intentionally honor him by continuing to bravely embrace his ripple of contrarian thinking in all my future writing.

In many ways, this concept of ripples is what's called the "butterfly effect."

It's the idea that even a tiny action, like the flap of a butterfly's wings, can ripple out into the world, creating unseen but significant results. It doesn't even take a grand gesture to make an impact. Even small, everyday choices can start a ripple effect.

Imagine this:

You're at a café, and the barista slaps down your latte on the counter in an angry way. You pause. You decide to hold back your urge to grumble, grab, and go.

Instead you say to the barista, "Rough morning, huh?"

She looks up, surprised maybe that anyone noticed or cared.

"Is it that obvious?" she asks, with a half smile.

"Only to the highly trained eye," you say, which earns a real, albeit brief, laugh.

You both exchange a few gripes about waking up early and the perpetual out-of-milk situation. Nothing groundbreaking, but there's a flicker, something like relief, in her expression.

Later, when this barista returns home, she'll listen a little more patiently as her son rants about his tyrannical third grade teacher. Maybe she'll laugh more freely, her heart a little lighter, when he dramatically collapses into his spaghetti dinner, pretending to be poisoned. And then they will have a tickle fight instead of the usual pre-bedtime grumble. And when she tucks him in, she will tell him an extra story.

The lesson?

When you choose to live by key core values—like kindness, patience, empathy, etc.—you wind up creating ripples ... which are spread to all who you encounter, then all who encounter them, then all who encounter them, and so on.

These ripples are your mini legacies.

I know that the word "legacy" usually conjures up images of grandeur, of names etched in the annals of history. But the truth is, not everyone is going to be a Martin Luther King Jr. or a Marie Curie. And that's okay! Because you don't have to change the world on a grand global scale to leave a meaningful legacy.

In fact, often the most fulfilling legacies aren't based on grandeur at all.

Your legacies don't have to do with status, power, fame, or fortune. They can simply be about the lives you touched, the people you inspired, and the changes you instigated—in your own unique way.

These mini legacies are the beautiful ripples you leave in the world—your everyday actions that wind up inspiring others in some way.

You can create these mini-legacy ripples whenever you choose to do small habits based in positive core values.

- When you choose to talk kindly to your barista
- When you decide to send an empathic email to your coworker
- When you lovingly handle a disagreement with your spouse
- When you listen actively to your screaming child instead of instantly yelling back

So when you consider your legacy, consider your mini legacies and the core values you show in your everyday actions.

The big takeaway?

When a loved one passes, I encourage you to intentionally think about their top core values and the ripples they left behind. It's a way to keep your loved one alive, metaphorically. And a way to honor the life they lived.

Take time to ask yourself:

- What key core values did your loved one embrace the most?
- How did their core values wind up creating ripples into your life or influence you in some way?

When you take the time to mindfully reflect on the ripples your departed loved ones left behind, you'll find a treasure trove of lessons.

- Perhaps they taught you about relentless optimism, even in the face of adversity.
- Maybe you were inspired by their ability to forgive and extend kindness, even when it wasn't noticeably deserved.
- Perhaps they motivated you to enjoy a love for books, a penchant for spontaneous road trips, or a stubborn refusal to apologize for loving what you love, however uncool it might be.

Now, let's not skip over the glaringly obvious.

Some of us have had to deal with some pretty dark characters, people who were abusive, narcissistic, or just perpetually checked out. You know, the kind of people who make you think, "Yep, that's my blueprint for what *not* to do." Their lives weren't just messy; they were full-on cautionary tales, complete with flashing neon signs screaming, "AVOID THIS."

These people left a different version of ripples . . .

- Maybe dealing with a workaholic parent showed you the value of a work/life balance.
- Perhaps the coldness of a narcissistic guardian taught you to value empathy.
- Or the inconsistency of an absent figure might have ingrained in you the importance of being there, really being present.
- Maybe you learned about boundaries from someone who respected none.
- Maybe you learned to keep your chin up when the chips were down because they never did.

So if your inherited legacy feels more like a curse, flip it. Make it your legacy to stop the family legacy. Build a life that corrects those errors, that shines not because it's free of blemishes, but because you chose to learn from everything and create something better.

As you reflect on all of these potential ripples, both positive and negative, remember:

The impact of those who pass doesn't end with their last breath. Their impact evolves. And if you allow it, their impact can inspire you to live more fully, love people more fiercely, enthusiastically prioritize time more vigilantly—and perhaps, *just perhaps*, die with fewer regrets.

Death, while a profound loss, can also become a profound invitation.

It can invite you to live more consciously, to align your actions with your deepest values.

It's like getting a spiritual defibrillation.

Your heart is jolted wider awake, and you find yourself on the path to wanting to live better. There's actually a term for this wake-up call that people experience after the death of a loved one.

POST-TRAUMATIC GROWTH (PTG)

Psychologists Richard Tedeschi and Lawrence Calhoun coined this term in the mid-'90s. PTG refers to the positive psychological growth experienced after the death of someone you love—or after any adversity.

PTG is a real, observable phenomenon—backed by a wide range of research studies—and includes positive changes like:

• Enhanced personal strengths
• Deeper relationships
• Increased appreciation for life
• Greater personal resilience
• A more meaningful spiritual or religious life
• Exploring new paths and possibilities

Why does post-traumatic growth happen?

Because death (or any kind of trauma) creates a massive "pattern interrupt" of your thoughts and beliefs. It shakes the very foundations you've built your life upon. As a result, PTG can become a catalyst for a "life-awakening time," motivating you to think and live in profoundly better ways.

In a way, post-traumatic growth after the death of a loved one isn't simply about bouncing back. It's about bouncing forward. It's about taking all that pain and turning it into something that shapes you into a better, stronger, more badass version of yourself.

So, here's the paradox:
- The death of a loved one can be devastating.
- Yet it can set the stage for your profound personal development.

Two Important Reminders

1. Growth after the death of a loved one is optional. It doesn't happen automatically. This ripple of growth requires you to engage actively with your grief, to question, to reflect. And yes, it hurts, but it also heals. You just need to mine your loss for golden nuggets (aka pebbles and ripples), then consciously weaves those pebbles and ripples into your story of growth.

2. Healing is not overnight. It happens gradually, as you navigate through the fog of loss. There's no express elevator or secret passageway that bypasses the messiness of mourning. It's a complicated journey through denial, anger, bargaining, depression, and acceptance. It feels less like a dignified progression and more like being stuck on the world's most heartbreaking roller-coaster ride, where the safety harness seems questionable at best.

So, if you're trying to rush through grief in search of some immediate silver lining, then you've taken a wrong turn somewhere between anger and bargaining. And you need to double back. Because you can't heal what you refuse to feel.

How do you tap into post-traumatic growth in a healthy and realistic way?
1. **Embrace the suck.** Acknowledge your pain. You can't gloss over it.
2. **You've got to face it**, head-on, like the brave (and slightly terrified) human you are.
3. **Bravely reflect.** Ask the hard questions. What does this loss mean to you? How has the way your loved one lived their life changed your view of the world?
4. **Redefine your narrative.** What core values did your loved one embody that left ripples in your life? How can you take those ripples and use them to live better?

5. **Experiment with new paths.** Loss can be a catalyst for change. Try something new. Take a risk. Use this opportunity to honor the lessons they shared with you by weaving them into your life.

In the next chapter, we're going to dive into your ripples—the ones you're making now and hope to leave behind.

First we're going to help you get clearer on your top core values.

Then we're going to chisel down your number one core value into your *epitaph* . . . which you can use as a mission statement for your life.

Yep, you heard me. We're going to write *your epitaph!*

Together we will write something snappy, fun, and inspiring—something that feels so much like you, it's as if you've been saying it all your life.

13

CRAFTING AN EPITAPH FOR A LIFE WELL LIVED

So, here we are. You're alive, sitting in your favorite chair, and now I'm asking you to think about what you might want as an epitaph when you're dead.

Fun, right?

For the uninitiated, an epitaph is basically a snappy short phrase or statement meant to sum up a person's life, usually carved onto their tombstone. Think of it as your one-liner for eternity. (No pressure.)

I know, writing an epitaph sounds like you're drafting some kind of morbid Hallmark card. "Dear Death, thanks for the memories!"

The truth is, nobody wakes up in the morning, brushes their teeth, and says, "Today feels like a good day to workshop my death slogan."

But hear me out: Writing your epitaph now, while you're still breathing, is more useful than you might guess.

An epitaph, when you think about it, is just a slogan for your life.

- Nike has *"Just Do It."*
- Apple proudly said, *"Think Different."*
- And you? You'll now have your very own epitaph to serve as your life's brand statement, a catchy tagline capturing what your life stands for.

The goal here is simple: Write a memorable sentence (or two), sprinkled with key core values and your vision for an ideal life.

Once you've written it, I'll explain how to use it as a handy mantra—something to remind yourself to live more boldly and authentically.

I've written my own epitaph, and I use it regularly—sort of like how a coach uses a whistle during practice. I whip it out when I need to stop myself from doing something "off-brand" for my life's mission.

And that's the real point: Your epitaph isn't just about how you want to be remembered later. It's about how you want to *show up* right now. Think of it as a to-do list for your soul, but shorter. And without the "buy almond milk" part.

Here Are The Five Big Perks of Writing Your Epitaph

1. Clear-Cut Goals

Researcher Gail Matthews, from Dominican University of California, found that people who jot down their goals were significantly more likely to achieve them. So writing your epitaph is a helpful goal-setter-and-getter.

2. Daily Thought Anchor

In the hustle and bustle of daily life, it's easy to get lost in petty concerns and short-term goals. But with your epitaph snug in your back pocket, it's like having a mental Post-it note, reminding you to focus on the big picture.

3. Authentic Living

This is your chance to carve out your life's values on your terms—forget society's expectations or Uncle Eric's two cents. Just focus on your beliefs.

4. Self-Fulfilling Prophecy

Your epitaph isn't just a fancy sentence. It's a blueprint for your life. Pick a virtue like "generosity," write an epitaph about it, and suddenly you'll find yourself more motivated to help neighbors or donate bucks to your favorite cause. Soon your actions will start to line up with your words.

5. Faster Than Reading Your Aspirational Eulogy

Your epitaph is like a speedy one-liner of your aspirational eulogy. It's short, to the point, and most importantly, it's something you can actually remember in the heat of the moment.

For example, imagine you're in a fight with your partner. You're not going to say, "Hold on, babe, let me grab my eulogy real quick and make sure yelling about your laundry habits aligns with my vision for my life."

Your epitaph is like a quick espresso shot of self-awareness.

Okay, enough preamble. Let's get started . . .

SO, HOW DO YOU CHISEL OUT AN EPITAPH?

Good question. After all, there was no "Epitaph Writing 101" back in school. But don't worry. I've got tools to help.

First up: a list of twenty thought-provoking writing prompts. You don't have to answer all of them. Just home in on the ones that spark something in you. Don't overthink it. Just scribble down your answers in "sloppy copy." You can tidy it all up later.

Oh, and if you're someone who freezes up the moment a blank page stares back at you—don't stress. I've also got a list of ready-made, pre-written epitaphs coming up.

But if you'd like to experiment with writing your own, you'll love these prompts. So, find a pen, your journal, and a cozy spot to sit. Maybe grab a glass of something nice. I'm thinking an iced latte with just a hint of vanilla. But it could be a bourbon with no ice—if you're really leaning into the whole "reflecting on mortality" thing.

One small thing: When you're done, close your journal. Firmly. You don't want to cause temporary shock to any loved ones who discover your rough epitaph drafts lying around.

Twenty Epitaph Writing Prompts

1. If someone could turn your life into a book or a movie, what would it be called?
2. What's the best compliment you've ever received?
3. If you had to leave one lasting piece of advice for the next generation, what would it be?
4. If there were an award named after you, what would it be for?
5. What song lyric would you use to describe your philosophy on life?
6. If your life were a metaphor, what would the metaphor be?
7. If you had to give a graduation speech about your life's mistakes, what would be your key message?
8. What would the warning label on your life say?
9. Imagine writing and designing a motivational quote poster about your life philosophy. What would it say?

10. When have you felt the most alive? What were you doing, and what core value is associated with this?

11. Think of a moment when you made a difficult choice. What one or two key core values guided you?

12. Describe a moment when you felt like a hero. What did you do, and how did this action align with your values?

13. Who are your heroes, and what qualities do they have that you strive to embody?

14. What do you wish more people in the world cared about?

15. What legacy do you want to leave that you're actively working toward right now?

16. Think of a time you failed spectacularly. What did you learn?

17. What's the most important thing you've ever said to someone?

18. What would your nemesis praise about you at your funeral?

19. What's the life lesson you'd emboss on a T-shirt to inspire strangers as you walk by?

20. If you could write a thank-you note to a challenge in your life, what would it say?

If You've Made It to This Sentence, Congrats!

Chances are this means that you've spent some quality time pondering those twenty thought starters and jotting down some catchy gravestone ideas. Now it's time to take those sprawling, messy responses and whittle them down into something punchy—your very own epitaph—doubling as your life's mission statement.

Remember: Your epitaph should ideally be succinct yet profound. Short but oh-so-mighty. Take a look at your sloppy copy and explore how you can chop and prune things until you're left with just a phrase (or two) that packs a punch.

Right now you might be thinking, "Karen, puh-lease! You make it sound simple—but how the heck do I do this?"

Let me help you out here.

First of all, don't worry about making it perfect. The goal isn't to sound like a philosopher. It's to sound like you ... figuring your sh*t out ... in real time.

Take your answers, start combining them, smash them together into sentences, and see what happens. Seriously, it's like making a sandwich with whatever's in your fridge. It doesn't have to look pretty. It just has to taste good.

And if you really want to get weird with it, write your answers on little scraps of paper and mix and match them like some kind of freaky life jigsaw puzzle. Sometimes random connections lead to the best realizations.

Still stuck on what your epitaph is? Review your top core values!

Remember those core values you've been brainstorming in past chapters? Well, now's a good time to review what you've written down. Yes, this is the beauty of writing things down. Your core values are just sitting there, waiting for you to rediscover them, like a pair of socks hidden in the dryer.

Still stuck? Not a problem, because . . .

As mentioned, I have a no-fail backup plan for you—my list of forty-five pre-made and ready-to-use epitaphs, categorized according to core values.

Fifteen Core Values and Their Potential Epitaphs

1. Authenticity
- Genuine to the core, even when it was inconvenient. Especially then.
- Wore their quirkiness and differences like badges of honor.
- Their unique ways made a dent in the universe.

2. Empathy
- Healed others with their words and presence.
- Their heart was a compass that pointed toward helping others.
- Their empathy was a bridge connecting disparate shores.

3. Determination
- Turned can'ts into cans and dreams into plans.
- Their grit forged paths where none existed.
- Danced through life's storms.

4. Innovation
- Turned "what if" into "what is."
- Saw beyond the horizon and brought visions to life.
- Questioned the path well trodden, paved a few of their own.

5. Joy and Positivity
- Spread joy like confetti.
- Their presence was a happy melody that lingered on.
- Never lost a battle to doubt, forever the optimist.

6. Leadership
- Led by example, led with heart.
- A leader who lifted others with every step.
- Saw the best potential in people. And brought it out.

7. Love
- Loved deeply and lived passionately.
- Their heart was a home built for many to feel welcome in.
- Saw the glass half full. Refilled it for others.

8. Mindfulness
- Mindfulness was their mantra, peace their path.
- Savored life's every sip, cherished its every flavor.
- Collector of moments, not things.

9. Wisdom
- Listened with curiosity, shared wisdom without the lecture.
- Old soul, young heart, wise mind.
- Forever student, eternal teacher.

10. Generosity
- Shared their riches, be they material or of the heart.
- Lived giving, died beloved.
- Their spirit of giving left an indelible mark.

11. Bravery
- Faced life with courage. Won more than lost.
- Dared where others hesitated.
- A heart bold as lions, a spirit free as birds.

12. Humor and Fun

- Made life laugh with them, a feat even more impressive on bad days.
- Laughter was a favorite companion, humor a shield during tough times.
- Embraced all seasons of life with a smile.

13. Adventure

- Never settled, always sought.
- Adventurer at heart, sage in spirit.
- Lived life as a grand exploration.

14. Curiosity

- Asked, "Why?" until the very end. Now asking, "What's next?"
- A lifelong learner, an eternal explorer.
- Their mind traveled more than their feet, and both went everywhere.

15. Discernment

- Measured twice, cut once, and made a life well crafted.
- Picked their battles and their friends with equal care. Rarely mistaken.
- Filtered the noise. Focused on the music of life.

When you shop around in these pre-written epitaphs, feel free to mix, match, and modify! Personalize and polish your epitaph phrase—until it becomes you-ier.

Your mission: When you read your epitaph mantra to your bestie, they will nod, smile, and say, "Yes, that's sooooooo you."

In fact, I recommend you grab your top epitaph options and run them by someone who knows you well. Ask them, "Which one sounds the most like me?" You might be surprised by their take.

But sharing is optional. You can keep your epitaph private, as something you repeat silently to yourself when life gets messy.

Curious what my epitaph is? I chiseled out this one . . .

"Love was the bread and butter of her life."

Why? Because empathic love is at the top of my core values list. I don't believe life is about who has the most stuff. It's about how well you love and are loved back. And so I lean on this epitaph mantra as my daily compass.

For example . . .

Let's say I'm knee-deep in writing this chapter, and my son pops in asking to walk the dogs together.

My first thought is, "Yeesh, I'm swamped with work."

But then my epitaph whispers in my ear, *"Love was the bread and butter of her life."*

That's my cue. Boom, my perspective shifts. I'm reminded how love is not just about feeling love. It's about showing love too. So, I tell him, "Give me ten, and I'm all yours."

That's the magic of having an epitaph. It's not just some line you slap on a headstone later. It's a tool for *now*. It's the tiny moral referee in your head, throwing up a flag when you're about to screw up and forget what really matters.

Because here's the truth: Most of us don't mess up our lives with huge, epic failures. We mess them up with small, stupid choices we make every day—because we forget what's important. An epitaph fixes that. It's a one-liner that calls you out—gently but firmly—so you don't lose sight of the big picture.

Now, it's your turn . . .

HOW TO LIVE UP TO YOUR EPITAPH

Writing a meaningful epitaph might have felt a bit tough. But here comes the bigger challenge: actually living up to it. After all, no one wants their epitaph to be the punchline to their life story.

Here's how to keep that from happening.

Reflect Regularly: Read your epitaph often, especially when you're at a crossroads. Think of it as your Mortality Morality Compass. It's a quick way to ask yourself, "Would Epitaph Me approve of this choice? Or would Epitaph Me be horrified, muttering, 'Well, there goes *that* dream'?"

Make It Visible: Put your epitaph on a Post-it. Set it as your phone wallpaper, or print it on a coffee mug or T-shirt. Picture yourself in the grocery store, wearing a shirt that says, "Say what you mean. Wear what you want." or "Life is short. Don't leave here with a boring story!" This is your chance to tell the world, "This is what I am all about!"

That said, you don't *have* to make it a public declaration. If the idea of people reading your life motto while you're buying eggs makes you queasy, then keep it private.

In Summary

Life's short. Your epitaph is even shorter. Make both count.

Next up, I have a special mortality tool that will help you to zero in on what truly matters to you. I'm about to introduce you to a "life audit." Think of it as being the head bouncer at the Nightclub of Your Life. Your job is to kick out the time-wasters and energy vampires trying to sneak past the velvet rope.

Get ready to declutter your days and stop squandering your precious, finite time.

14

LIFE AUDIT:
GETTING RID OF YOUR CRAP AND CLUTTER

"I didn't have enough time."

We've all used that excuse, haven't we? It's the grown-up remix of "the dog ate my homework." And it's the ultimate adult cop-out.

Let's get real. Complaining that we don't have enough time is basically our go-to excuse for not wanting to admit, "I just didn't make it a priority."

So, here's a thought experiment:

If time were money, would you be as cavalier about where and how you spent it? Or would you be a bit more Scrooge-like with your precious time?

Chances are your time management skills would take a swift turn for the better . . . if time were actually cold, hard cash. You'd suddenly become a Time Spendthrift.

Unfortunately, many of us are like oblivious so-called Time Millionaires on the verge of going bankrupt, because we're not keeping track of where our time is going.

This is bizarre when you pause to think about it. After all, you put in the effort to protect your cars, your diamond jewelry, your home. When you fail to guard your time, it's as if you're leaving your front door wide open with a neon sign flashing, "Free stuff! Come grab as much of my time as you want!"

Now, you might be thinking, "Not me, I'm only swamped with very important stuff."

But let's be real. If you tally up all the hours spent in the black hole of social media, channel surfing, or just plain zoning out, you'd probably find lots of wasted hours.

I get it. I've been there too. One minute I'm watching a cooking show. And the next thing I know, it's midnight and I haven't moved for five hours.

You know what would be great?

If Netflix stopped asking, "Are you still watching?" and instead asked, "Hey buddy, is this really how you want to be spending your time?" That might just snap us out of our binge-watching coma—and make us wake up to the stark fact that every Netflix binge is a choice against, say, writing that novel or calling an old friend.

Because if we want to live a truly fulfilling life, we've got to cut the crap and make room for the stuff that truly counts. Yet most of us cruise through our days on autopilot. We blink, then somehow another week, month, year slips by. And all the epic stuff we planned? Still not done.

Yep, time is a relentless, merciless jerk. It marches on, indifferent to your pleas for "Just five more minutes!" Before you know it, you hit a certain age, look back, and wonder, "What the heck was I doing with my time?"

THE HUMAN CAPACITY FOR TIME DENIAL

Isn't it wild how we all just collectively decide to ignore that time is ticking away? This has been going on for eons now.

In fact, way back (in 4 BCE-ish to 65 CE-ish), the philosopher Seneca threw out this zinger:

> It's not that we have a short time to live, but that we waste a lot of it. Life is long enough, and it has been given in sufficiently generous measure to allow the accomplishment of the very greatest things if the whole of it is well invested.

Translation: If we actually paid attention to our lives, we'd find we have enough time to do everything we want.

Admittedly, our world has accelerated since Seneca's time, thanks to the addition of our supposedly time-saving inventions. Like the internet that ensnares more than it frees, smartphones that tether rather than liberate, social media that isolates more than it connects, and Zoom meetings that stretch, elastic and endless.

Ironically, these inventions, meant to save us time, have instead devoured it. They promised liberation and delivered a new kind of bondage, making us servants to the beep, the buzz, and the blink—and distracting us from what actually matters.

All of this reminds me of something profound that author Sogyal Rinpoche wrote about in *The Tibetan Book of Living and Dying*. He shared how he believed we humans have a tendency to compulsively cram our lives with a myriad of unimportant activities, leaving little time to confront what matters most.

Rinpoche cleverly called this habit "active laziness." And he jokingly renamed all of the petty projects we refer to as our "responsibilities" as our "irresponsiblities."

Plus, Rinpoche warned that if we're not careful, we can get so caught up in busying our days with total nonsense that we become "unconscious living corpses"— sleepwalking through our days on this planet—never going after our truest desires.

What Rinpoche described reminds me of something powerful that the author Milan Kundera philosophized about in his book *Slowness,* a slender volume I ironically sped through in a night. Kundera explained how we live in a highly sped-up culture, and that our need for speed promotes forgetting.

For example:
- If you want to forget something, you will pick up speed walking down the street.
- If you want to remember something, you'll slow down your steps.

Kundera warned how speeding up your life keeps you from remembering daily details like, "Oops! Forgot to pick up more milk!" Or worst: "Oops! Forgot to be my best kind, listening self!"

Meaning?

The next time you find yourself racing down the street to go to your next big appointment, know that you're not only running to your appointment. You are literally running from contact with your truest feelings, deepest needs, and most valuable insights.

The solution?

We need to stop getting caught up in this speed trap—by setting up speed bumps in our daily life to pause and reflect.

Listen, I know this chapter is starting to sound like a particularly aggressive therapy session, but I'm gonna keep saying it again and again.

Your time here is limited.

While that thought might cause a knot in your stomach, it can actually be very liberating. You see, once you acknowledge that your time is finite, you start to recognize that every second you're arguing with a troll on the internet, or binge-watching a show you don't even like, or staying in a job (or relationship) that makes you miserable . . . is a second you're never getting back.

Best of all, when you start to live more mindfully, you not only save time, you save energy too. Suddenly you stop feeling burnt out, so you actually enjoy life more.

Otherwise, if you're busy all the time, it's like running a marathon—then being too exhausted to enjoy that free banana that you get at the finish line. And believe me, everyone deserves to enjoy their metaphorical life banana, whether that's reveling in deep, meaningful relationships, indulging in a fun hobby, or doing anything that makes you feel like you're thriving, not just existing.

With this in mind, here's a fun metaphor to help you smarten up about how you use your time.

Think of Your Life Like a Buffet

Just because everything is available to eat doesn't mean you need to stuff your plate. You need to select from the buffet wisely.

If you want to find more time in your life . . .
- You must recognize what matters most, then heap that onto your life's plate.
- Plus, you must recognize the junky stuff, then skip it entirely.

With this in mind, I recommend you do a life audit to identify the crap and clutter in your daily life.

Admittedly the word "audit" might sound like something you'd want to avoid—as much as death itself. But stick with me here, because I'm about to introduce a new version of an audit—one that will wildly improve your life.

In this life audit we're going to do some time accounting.

This involves answering some thought-provoking questions, from pinpointing your time-consuming activities, to identifying the parts of your life that feel more like obligations than choices.

This isn't about beating yourself up and spiraling into guilt. No, this is about identifying your Time Leaks—so you can stop them from turning into Happiness Leaks.

As Albert Camus, that cheeky French philosopher, once said, "Real generosity towards the future lies in giving all to the present."

So that's what I want you to do. Focus on amping up your present.

I want you to shine a light on how you can play the game of life more effectively. Find where your life needs a little tweaking. Maybe even a lot. Then edit away at these problematic areas.

Now it's time for me to mention the big star of this intervention: mortality awareness.

Death is a persuasive time management motivator because it works like a nagging little voice saying, *"Hey, remember me? Death? Yeah, I'm an actual thing. And you don't have all the time in the world, pal."*

The good news: By now, you've read a good chunk of this book, so your brain's been marinating in thoughts about how temporary your life is. At this point, you're actually ready—maybe even excited—to start cutting out the crap and zeroing in on the stuff that actually matters.

Trust me, if you do this life audit right, later on, when you're an old geezer, you'll not only be loaded up with inspiring stories to tell, you'll also have a strikingly short list of regrets to whine about.

SIXTEEN LIFE AUDIT QUESTIONS TO PONDER

Ready to dive deep? Grab your journal and let's shake things up with these life audit questions. No wrong answers here, just your raw, unfiltered thoughts spilling out!

1. What activities waste your time the most, and why do you keep doing them?
2. What significant project or ambition have you been postponing? How can you schedule time for it now?
3. What activities engage you deeply and make time fly? How can you do more of these?
4. Do your daily tasks help you achieve your long-term goals? If not, what changes are needed?
5. How often do you participate in activities that genuinely refresh you?
6. What tasks can you delegate or eliminate to free more time for important activities?
7. Are you truly productive—or just busy? How can you better differentiate the two?
8. Does your screen time overshadow the time spent on personal growth or with loved ones?
9. What would you attempt today if you were 50 percent braver or guaranteed success?
10. Which tasks and people exhaust and drain you the most and why? What can you change?
11. Do parts of your life feel obligatory rather than chosen? How can you alter this?
12. What habits do you have that detract from your well-being or personal growth?
13. In what ways do you compromise your needs to satisfy others?
14. What fears or doubts prevent you from pursuing your passions?
15. If your life ended tomorrow, what would be your biggest regret? What can you do about it today?
16. What are your financial goals, and are you on track to meet them?

Done? How are you feeling? Did you become a bit more aware of the clutter clogging up your life?

Admittedly, these questions might lead you to think, "You know what, I'll answer these questions tomorrow."

I hope that's not you! Because tomorrow is not a guarantee.

I mean, we've covered this, right?

So this life audit? It's kinda not just a suggestion. It's a blaring wake-up call screaming, "Stop acting like you've got all the time in the world and start crafting a life you're jazzed about . . . like, yesterday!"

Bolster up your core value of bravery—and jot down some answers to those sixteen questions. It's time to stop dressing up your soul-sucking habits with (b)lame excuses and pain-softening rationalizations.

When You're Done, Here's What to Do Next

First, separate your crap and clutter according to the degree of difficulty it will take to fix them, like you're sorting laundry. Just as you separate lights from darks, you'll want to figure out which habits need a gentle washing—and which ones require a heavier cycle of cleansing.

And then, consider how your habits might fit into these three categories: Life Drains, Happiness Leaks, and Life Wasters.

Yep, I urge you to vilify your crap and clutter habits—thoroughly! After all, these are your time demons . . . and it's time to send them back to wherever time demons come from.

HERE'S HOW TO IDENTIFY YOUR TIME DEMONS

Life Drains: These are the people, habits, or tasks that suck the life out of you like an energy vampire. Like that friend who dumps their problems on you, then says, "Anyway, gotta run!" Or your compulsion to check work emails at 2 AM instead of sleeping like a normal human being.

How to handle: You gotta shut down these energy-suckers before they get their fangs into you. Maybe tell your cousin you're not available for their latest drama, or speak up to that friend who only texts you when they need something. Keep the phone or laptop out of the bedroom or in a drawer after 8 PM.

Happiness Leaks: These are the easiest to spot because they're so dumb, it's almost impressive. Like spending forty-five minutes reading about ancient Roman sewer systems. Or hanging out in the kitchen snacking, thinking, "Just one more chip" while your responsibilities collect dust. You know you've been drained by a Happiness Leak when you find yourself wondering, "Why do I feel so unsatisfied all the time?" Spoiler alert: It's because you've spent three hours a day scrolling through Instagram, drooling over other people's vacations instead of planning your own! Every little mindless routine, like rewatching the same crappy sitcom, has a cumulative effect, leaving you wondering why life feels so *meh.*

How to handle: Patch those leaks. Catch yourself mid-scroll and replace the habit with something that makes you feel good. Plan your own vacation instead of drooling over someone else's. Read a book. Take a walk. Do a habit from your To-Die List.

Life Wasters: Now, these are the big, soul-sucking liabilities. The job you hate but stay in. The relationship that feels like Stockholm syndrome. These aren't just little leaks. These are black holes swallowing your best years.

How to handle: Start cutting the dead weight. If a job feels like a prison sentence, make plans to escape. If certain people drain your energy, limit your time with them. Embrace the discomfort of change. Ask yourself, what's worse? The temporary pain of making a tough decision or the long-term regret of staying stuck?

Dealing with tough-to-remove time demons?

Sometimes your time demons get so knotted into your routine that trying to extract them is like untangling a plate of spaghetti.

But fear not. In the next chapter, I'll be equipping you with a full arsenal of power tools, specifically tailored to exterminate those tough-to-remove time wasters.

Think of it as pest control for your productivity. We're about to go full exterminator on your regrets.

15

SIX TICK-TOCK TAMERS: IT'S TIME TO TAKE CONTROL OF YOUR TIME

Life is funny. You start out with all these grand plans—you're going to write a novel, run a marathon, adopt a dog, maybe even learn Italian. Then, before you know it, you're three seasons deep into a Netflix show you don't even like, or scrolling through your phone like there's going to be a pop quiz on cat memes . . . *and you've accomplished bupkis!*

Bad habits are sneaky like that. They sidle up to you, whispering, *"It's just ten minutes, what's the harm?"* And before long, those ten minutes have turned into ten years, and you're still waiting for your "someday" to arrive. Worse, these habits start to feel like part of your personality—like you'd be betraying yourself if you stopped.

But here's the thing:

Many of the most fulfilling parts of your life are not nestled in your comfort zone.

They're out there—on the other side of it—waving frantically, trying to get your attention.

No worries. I'm about to introduce you to six powerful time management tools, crafted to dismantle the cozy prison of your bad time habits.

TOOL ONE: THE MORTALITY AWARENESS MONTHLY MARBLE JAR

Yep, it sounds like a prop from a gothic novel. And in a way, it is.

Here's how it works: You're going to fill a big glass jar with a bunch of marbles. Each marble represents one month out of the (estimated) time you have left to live.

- If you're 50 years old right now, then I want you to optimistically shoot for living to 100. That leaves you with 600 months. So purchase 600 marbles.
- If you're 30 and equally hopeful to live to 100, you're looking at 840 months to go. So purchase 840 marbles.
- Or simply do the math for whatever age you are!

Whatever your age, you'll need a big jar for this.

- If you're a 600-marble person, get a jar around 32 fluid ounces.
- If you're an 840-marble person, aim for something like 42 fluid ounces.
- Based on those numbers, estimate the jar size for whatever age you are.

Each month, I want you to take one marble out of the jar. Then, as the months go by, watch as the marbles gradually decrease.

What's incredibly powerful—and kinda scary—about this jar is how it will make the abstract concept of time very painfully real. You will literally see your months slipping away, decreasing one marble at a time. Let me tell you, nothing makes you reconsider your life choices quite like watching your allotted marbles disappear.

But this jar isn't just meant to be a reminder that time is passing. It's meant to be a catalyst for action.

So I want you to make removing each marble a ritual. Maybe do it over a glass of wine on the first evening of every month. Or over a coffee during the first morning of a new month.

As you remove each marble, think about how you spent the past month. Take time to ask yourself:

- Was this month well spent?
- Did you waste it on the crap and clutter?
- Or did you invest your time in things that enrich your life?

This jar of marbles will be a powerful wake-up call. It will poke you in the ribs, gently or not so gently, every time you remove a marble. Because you'll begin to realize just how much every action—or inaction—truly counts.

TOOL TWO: THE ANTI-SLEEPWALKING AID

Remember in a prior chapter how the author Rinpoche warned people that if we're not careful, we can become like living corpses, sleepwalking through life?

Well, I have an anti-sleepwalking aid. I want you to set alarms on your phone to go off randomly in your day. Set them for various quirky times. For example: 10:11 AM, 1:27 PM, 4:38 PM, 8:12 PM.

The goal: Catch yourself off guard, so the alarm ring becomes your speed bump in your busy day, getting you to pause and catch how you truly use your time.

At each pause, ask yourself one of the following four questions:

Question 1: If I were to die tomorrow, would I regret spending my time on the thing I am doing right now?

Why it helps: This is your future self giving you a gut check. Are you doing something you'd be proud of, or are you just mindlessly scrolling through your ex's vacation photos? Nothing clarifies your choices quite like the cold splash of thinking about your imminent nonexistence.

Question 2: How does this action I am doing right now contribute to my legacy—or stop me from attaining my legacy?

Why it helps: It empowers you to focus on the long game. It reminds you that each choice you make is a brick in the foundation of the legacy you're building. It gets you to become aware of your legacy construction—or legacy destruction. Which are you choosing?

Question 3: How is this habit I am choosing in this moment affecting not only me, but others in my life?

Why it helps: This question is about reading the room of your future. Every choice casts ripples—it gets you to think about where they extend. This question helps you to stop being accidentally selfish and start considering how your habits affect others. Think of it as doing a cost-benefit analysis but with a moral twist.

Question 4: How does this habit I am choosing in this moment align with my top core values—or does it?

Why it helps: This question forces you to notice if you are living a life that's true to your core values, or if you are living a lie. Your values should guide your actions. If there's a disconnect, this question will be your bullshit detector—letting you know something's off and it's time to recalibrate—so you can craft a life you're proud of.

There you go. Your anti-sleepwalking aids, in the form of four alarmingly insightful questions! Set those random alarms. Let them be unexpected nudges throughout your day. You might just be surprised at what you find out about yourself and how you're spending your time.

You can also use these questions whenever you're at a crossroads in your day to help you decide what to do next.

Speaking of crossroads, our next tool will mindfully help you to decide how to set your priorities so you'll always know what to do first—and what to do never.

TOOL THREE: THE EISENHOWER MATRIX

This is a simple yet brilliant tool for decision-making. It's named after president Dwight D. Eisenhower. The story goes that he developed this handy tool to help him manage his time during World War II . . . because, you know, a wrong decision in wartime can lead to major disaster.

The next time you're swamped with too many tasks on your agenda, I want you to pull out the Eisenhower matrix. It works like clearing the fog off your glasses. Suddenly, you'll see what you need to do, delegate, delay, or dump!

The Eisenhower matrix classifies your tasks into four quadrants. It's a simple 2 x 2 grid with the columns labeled "Urgent" and "Not Urgent" and the rows labeled "Important" and "Not Important."

	URGENT	NOT URGENT
IMPORTANT	1	2
NOT IMPORTANT	3	4

Every "do" that's due on your to-do list fits into one of these four quadrants, like so:

Quadrant 1: Urgent and Important—Do It Like Your Hair's on Fire

These are your "must do now" fire-alarm tasks. Crises, last-minute deadlines, health scares—these bad boys need your attention, like, yesterday. Deal with them first . . . or you're toast.

Quadrant 2: Not Urgent but Important—the Art of Slow Cooking

This quadrant includes tasks that are super important, but don't have screaming deadlines. Learning Italian. Writing that novel. Scheduling that yearly checkup so you don't end up in Quadrant 1 later. This is also where your To-Die List lives. You need to schedule these tasks, then do them slowly over time. They're the pot roast of productivity—low heat, long cook, incredible results.

Quadrant 3: Urgent but Not Important—Delegate Like a Boss

The tasks in this box need to get done now. But they don't need your personal touch. These are chores you can outsource. Paying bills? Set up autopay. Grocery shopping? Delivery exists. Think of it this way: Every time you're wasting energy on Quadrant 3 crap, you're stealing time from something that actually matters—like being with your family or, I don't know, *enjoying your life*. So delegate it. Outsource it. Pass it off. Save yourself the hassle.

Quadrant 4: Neither Urgent Nor Important—Just Drop It!

This is pretty much the junk drawer of tasks. These are the activities you do in auto-pilot mode that don't really make your life any better. Scrolling through social media. Stressing about things you can't control. Browsing online shopping sites. This quadrant is a coffin where time vampires hang out, suck up your time, and give nothing back. You must drag them into the light and let them turn to dust.

I gotta say, I love using the Eisenhower matrix. It helps me to better curate my life.

Speaking of life curation, this brings me to the next time management tool.

TOOL FOUR: ENVISION YOURSELF
AS THE CURATOR OF YOUR LIFE

As you probably know, art curators are very discerning at what they choose to hang in their gallery. So, I want you think of yourself as a discerning curator of your life. But instead of paintings, you're choosing experiences, relationships, jobs, habits, hobbies—basically all the things that take up space in your limited, finite life.

It's a tough job. You can't choose everything—or your life gallery will become a garage sale of the mediocre. Plus you have limited resources, with only a certain amount of time, energy, and attention in your budget. So you must spend your budget only on things that inspire or enhance. Things that say, "This is important. It is beautiful. It is worth the time and space it takes up."

As a skilled curator, regret becomes less of a threat, because you choose very consciously. And so there are fewer "What was I thinking?" moments, and more "I remember why I chose this" moments.

I want you to own this identity as a discerning curator of your life . . . and so I created this handy-dandy "I am and so I do" statement for you to put on your To-Die List.

Your "I am and so I do" statement:

I am: A discerning curator of my life.

I do: And so I spend my precious time on things that matter most to Future Me.

When you embrace this "I am and so I do" statement, you'll find it easier to say that tongue twister of a word "no."

Plus here's another time management tool to help you become fluent in the language of no.

TOOL FIVE: SAY NO WITH THE SAME FREQUENCY
AS A TODDLER

The word "no" is more than a tiny two-letter word. It's a testament to self-respect. With this in mind, if someone or something doesn't dovetail with your core values, your life goals, or the person you aspire to be . . . you must reject it.

Remember: You can't pour from an empty cup, as fortune cookie wisdom reminds!

Best of all, when you begin saying no to time wasters, you will have far more space to fill up your cup with things that truly matter.

So, shed that people-pleaser costume and muster the courage to say no. Say it firmly, free of guilt or flimsy excuses. Start drawing clearer boundary lines in the sand. Or better yet, in the concrete. Because Aspirational Eulogy You is a badass like that.

Admittedly, saying no can be tough, especially when it involves manipulative, toxic people. But you must learn to prioritize yourself.

I believe that you can't fix toxic people. But thankfully you can control your exposure to them.

- Think of it like this: If life hands you lemons, by all means, make lemonade.
- But if life hands you a jug of sour, lemony people juice, maybe don't set up a lemonade stand!
- You have the power, the absolute veto, to declare, "This is not for my palate," and walk away.

Bonus: Five Ways to Say NO and Make It Stick

Use "I" statements. Make it about your needs. "I need to pass on this because I've committed to less screen time this evening." It's like telling someone you're allergic to shellfish when really, you just don't like it. Or feel free to white lie a little. "I have to decline because I'm already booked" is always valid, even if you're booked with a date with your couch and old episodes of *Murder, She Wrote.*

Keep it simple. Don't give them a novel. "No" is a complete sentence. The more you explain, the more they think you're leaving a door cracked open. Shut that door. Lock it.

Repeat if necessary. Some people hear "no" and think, "Challenge accepted." These people need a second helping of "no," served hot and firm.

Provide alternatives when possible. If you can't do something, maybe you know someone who can. "I can't make it to your sea-shanty-themed karaoke night, but have you tried inviting Jerry? He loves singing and questionable fashion choices."

Delay your response. Sometimes all you need is a little time to muster up that no. "Let me think about it and I'll get back to you" is a positive use of procrastination—and surprisingly effective.

With these strategies at your disposal, saying no will feel less like a taboo and more like a magic trick, one that makes anxiety disappear and replaces it with inner peace.

TOOL SIX: SHRINK NEGATIVITY INTO NUGGETIVITY

I'm wrapping up this list with one of my favorite time-saving tips! Every day when I wake up, I decide not to . . .

- Kick myself about past mistakes
- Whine about resentments
- Make lists in my head of all my regrets
- Count up all the people who let me down
- Continue to count on people who fill me with anxiety

Ever since I started enforcing these rules, I've magically found more hours in my day—hours I can spend doing more of what I love, with the people I love. Plus, I'm happier while I'm doing it.

How do I accomplish this negativity-shrinking? Simple. Whenever I'm feeling particularly curmudgeonly, I use a mindfulness tool I call "the stop and swap."

I call it this because when you're cranky, it's tough to simply halt negative thoughts in their tracks. Instead you need to also swap in some positively reframed thoughts to replace the negative ones!

Here's the logic of it . . .
- Let's say you wanted to stop a puppy from chewing on your slipper.
- You need to give the puppy something else to chew on—maybe a bone.
- After all, the puppy has this urge to chew on something.

- If you do NOT give the puppy something NEW to chew on, it will keep chewing the slipper.

When you're upset, your anxious mind has the urge to chew on something. If you simply only try to stop the negative thought—and don't also give your mind something new to chew—your mind will keep going back to chewing on your negative thoughts.

How to Do a Stop and Swap

- Write down your negative thoughts. (Or mentally get clear on them.)
- Brainstorm some positively reframed thoughts to serve as replacements.
- When a gloomy thought shows up . . . stop it by swapping in your newly reframed positive thought!

Examples:

- STOP thinking: "People don't like me."
- SWAP IN the reframe: "The right people appreciate me."
- STOP thinking: "I'm not reaching goals fast enough."
- SWAP IN the reframe: "Everything has its process. I'm right on time."
- STOP thinking: "Everything is going wrong."
- SWAP IN the reframe: "I focus 20 percent on the problem, 80 percent on the solutions."

This technique works because it's like being the DJ of your mental playlist. If a negative-thinking track starts playing, simply hit that mental reshuffle button. Stop it and swap it for a thought track that boosts your mood.

HOW TO USE THIS TIME-TAMING TOOL KIT

You don't have to go all in and adopt all six tools. But I'd definitely recommend you pick a few that resonate.

Please know: All these strategies have been instrumental in helping me personally get many important things done—including writing this very book!

I encourage you to test these tools out and take command of your time. Because how you spend your time . . . is essentially how you spend your life. And you don't want your epitaph to read "Here lies Susie, who spent an inordinate amount of time watching cat videos!"

Now that you've decluttered your schedule, next up you'll be organizing a different kind of mess . . . namely, the junky stuff you've hoarded over the years.

It's time to take a hard look in your closets and drawers and ask, "Do I really want to leave all this for someone else to sort out after I'm gone?" (As well as the timeless question: "Did I ever really need an avocado de-pitter?")

16

GRAVE DECISIONS: HOW TO DO A SWEDISH DEATH CLEANING

Want to live more intentionally? If so, I recommend you do a Swedish death cleaning. Yeah, you heard me. Death. Cleaning. Or feel free to call this process by its Swedish name, "döstädning," if you want to sound fancy and slightly intoxicated at your next cocktail party.

This decluttering system was pioneered by Margareta Magnusson, and it's meant to get you thinking, *If I pass away tomorrow, do I really want my kids finding my embarrassing stack of love letters from my high school fling?*

Basically, SDC is about confronting your mortality with a cleaning spree. You go through your stuff, decide what you want to get rid of and what you want to leave behind for others to deal with when you pass.

But this process is not just about trashing old concert tees or those DVDs you borrowed and never returned. It can also lead to a mental purge. Like, do you really need to hang on to that grudge from seventh grade gym class? Or all those petty little hurts and embarrassments? Probably not.

So, think of this process as a decluttering for your brain, like a group therapy session with your past selves. Because you'll also be reflecting a lot on who you've been and what you've done.

The end result?

You're not just cleaning; you're facing both your mortality and your life with a trash bag in hand.

I DID A SWEDISH DEATH CLEANING RECENTLY—
IT WAS ENLIGHTENING

I waded through those mountains of "what the hell was I thinking" purchases and those "I remember getting this in a fond way but geez that was eons ago and not relevant now" kinda items.

Then I mindfully kept only the things that mattered—the stuff that made me smile instead of cringe. The "I would save this from a burning house" kinda stuff.

How and why did I decide to do a Swedish death cleaning?

For me, it all started when I opened my closet and realized I had, no joke, seven black sweaters.

Seven.

I don't even wear black sweaters that much! I mean, what am I, a cat burglar? A mime in training? Steve Jobs? Why do I need seven?

And because I've been thinking about my mortality—and writing this book—it occurred to me:

When I die . . . do I really want people going through my closet and saying, "Wow, she really had a thing for black sweaters, huh?"

So here's what I did:

I grabbed a glass of wine (because let's be real, you need a drink for this kind of emotional upheaval), sat on the floor of my closet, and started sorting through things.

By the end of the day, I had four bags of clothes to donate, a closet I could actually see the back of, and only one black sweater—because, hey, let's not get crazy, a girl still needs one.

Want to try it? Here's the plan.

Step 1: Start with the Easy Stuff
(Clothes, Junk Drawers, and Random Crap)

Don't begin this process with the stuff that might make you cry—like love letters from your high school ex who's probably bald now. Start with the easy wins: clothes you haven't worn since 1998, the junk drawer full of random wires you swear you'll need someday but won't, and all those Tupperware lids that no longer have matching bottoms (or a Tupperware company to buy them from).

Step 2: Sort with Brutal Honesty (Would Anyone Want This Crap?)

Ask yourself: "If I kick the bucket tomorrow, would anyone want this junk?" If the answer is, "Hell no," into the donation bin it goes. And if it's something even Goodwill would reject? Trash it without mercy. Nobody's going to cherish your collection of expired soy sauce packets.

Step 3: Give Away the Good Stuff (or At Least What You *Think* Is Good)

That antique lamp you swear is worth something? Time to pass it on. Give things to people who might actually use them now. If nobody's interested, that's a sign. You're not leaving behind heirlooms. You're offloading a burden.

Step 4: Create a "Not Ready Yet" Box (For All the Emotional Baggage)

For those sentimental items that make your heart do that thing where you can't let go, create a "Not Ready Yet" box. You don't have to part with Grandma's porcelain cat collection right this second. You can deal with it later.

Step 5: Celebrate Your Wins (Seriously, It's Hard Work!)

This isn't easy, so celebrate when you make progress. Reward yourself with a cupcake or a bubble bath. You're clearing out your life—and that deserves a moment of triumph.

Now here's more of the inside scoop on what I discovered and learned.

WHAT I LEARNED

I started my Swedish death cleaning with the "fashion graveyard."

As mentioned, it all started with those seven black sweaters.

But afterward I dug deeper . . . and discovered some true fashion faux pas. Like my expensive red-bottomed high-heel Christian Louboutin shoes. Admittedly, at one time they were purchases of pride—until I realized they were instruments of torture. I remembered the many times I limped home barefoot.

Looking at them now was a glaring reminder of how when I was younger I'd willingly cripple myself in the name of beauty and social status.

As I dug deeper into the closet, I realized it was like a Museum of Pain.

- There was the Gucci pencil skirt from my pencil-thin era, when salads were meals and meals were negotiations.
- There were those skinny jeans that only zipped up once—the day I bought them.
- And don't get me started on that silk blouse that only fits if I don't breathe or eat carbs for a week.

Why did I do this to my younger self? Why did I try to squeeze my supposedly feminist self into these torture devices—just because society told me they were the epitome of cool?

It's ridiculous, and it's not just me. So many of us women spend half our lives (and income) trying to fit into tiny, fancy, designer clothes that were never meant for us, just to fit an image that's about as real as a unicorn.

What did I do? I thanked the shoes and clothes for their service . . . and for teaching me a painful lesson. Then I put them in a bag for Goodwill and said good riddance.

And So My First Death Cleaning Insight Had Arrived

I'm done torturing myself to meet societal expectations. I'm reclaiming my love for comfort. If that means a little less glam and a lot more sneakers, then so be it.

Next . . . I dug further into my closet and found some old clothes I still love—outfits that screamed, "This is me!" and, "Remember when!"

First up, there was my mother's vintage denim jacket. Its fabric still held the ghost of her wild days . . . and mine too.

Then there was my favorite sequined dress, because every girl needs her armor. This sparkly dress was my go-to confidence outfit for every make-or-break event.

Oh, and then there was an embroidered scarf, a gift from a dear friend who knew my penchant for the handmade and artisan. A reminder of what a spiritual sister she was to me.

And yessss . . . the black combat boots! Which I paired with everything from fancy gowns to jeans. They've walked me through black-tie events and dive-bar escapades—and marched me past exes with a swagger that said, "Eat your heart out." These boots have seen it all.

Next up, my favorite bright yellow coat, which shouts sunshine—and is an unofficial social catalyst, inspiring strangers to smile and tell me: "Love that jacket!"

I decided to keep all of these items, because they weren't just about fashion. They were my companions through the years, bookmarks of important memories, keepsakes of joys and jolts. Although they didn't solve problems, they sometimes made them feel a little less heavy.

This Brought Me to My Next Death Cleaning Insights

- You gotta find what grips tightly to your spirit—and understand why— so you can continue to treasure hunt more of it.
- It doesn't matter how old you are; the only thing a woman should ever stop wearing is other people's opinions.

Next up, after the fashion review came the process of letting go of decades' worth of journals, the kind I used to write in because someone once told me it was a good way to "find myself."

I unearthed a box in the back of my closet. It was taped with the resignation of a time capsule, meant for later—much later. But it was later now. I sliced the tape, and the flaps opened with a sigh, like an accordion breathing out decades-old air.

I slid out the first journal and opened to a random page: "Had coffee with an ex, made me miss the relationship. Then he spoke."

Just like that, I was laughing. Because some things never change. And sometimes those things are your exes. Plus, this entry was a reminder to appreciate my current, less dramatic, happy family life.

Another flip, another entry: "Sometimes, I think happiness is just the space between two sorrows." I checked the date. I was in my thirties. Yep, that's exactly how I remembered my thirties: a time of cynicism.

Near the back of the journal, a single line caught my eye. "I'm happy," I wrote on a day marked with no particular significance. Just a random Thursday, when happiness was notable enough to record, fleeting enough to fear its loss. I closed the journal. The snap of the cover felt like the closing of a door on a house I used to live in.

I dipped inside the box again. There were many more journals—each offering a different life chapter, a different me.

I opened a journal from my college days. First entry: "Accidentally made eye contact with my crush for 2.5 seconds. Will we have beautiful babies? Stay tuned." It's funny how back then, 2.5 seconds could fuel a whole day's worth of daydreaming.

I put the college journal away and grabbed a different one. First entry I flipped to: "Met a guy. He seems nice. Too nice. Is he a serial killer? Stay tuned." I found it charming how my past paranoia used to be kind of cute, and not like today's, which involves true threats like catfishing, stalking, and identity theft.

Next, I found an entry marked with a Post-it: "Plans for the summer: write a novel." I smiled fondly at those words, because I actually did do that.

I turned to another page, and I discovered a ticket stub pressed like a flower. It was from that concert I went to alone, armed with the stubborn independence of someone who needed to prove they could.

I closed the journal, then realized these entries were like little snippets of who I used to be. It's funny. I thought I'd just throw out all of these journals. But I wasn't ready. Inside this box, dozens more journals awaited. Each with their own stories, their own versions of me, a map of my evolution.

So I taped the box back up and stored it back in the closet. Reading the rest of the journals would wait. But for now, it was enough to know that they were there. And that I was there. But now I'm *here*.

This Brought Me to My Next Swedish Death Cleaning Insight

This process isn't just about ditching stuff. It's about celebrating the stuff that made me a me. It's about understanding that every silly, sad, or sappy moment contributed to the person I am today.

Next up . . . I decided to do a heave-ho of all those half-started "someday" projects that were just making me feel bad for never getting to them.

I found stacks of papers, some with just a few sentences for new business ideas. Plus I found half-started screenplays. Some that made me cringe and shred them. Others that made me want to keep tinkering with them. I made a note on my phone: Finish that sci-fi screenplay.

Next, I found boxes jam-packed with old hobbies: needlepointing kits, beading kits, watercoloring kits, like exhibits from The Museum of Half-Baked Dreams.

We all have them. Those projects that were going to change the world or at least change *our* world. They were shiny, full of promise, and now? They're dead weight.

So one by one, I plunked these relics into a giant trash bag. Because sometimes the bravest thing you can do is let go. And no, it's not about admitting defeat. It's about acknowledging that you've changed, and what mattered once doesn't fit who you are now.

This Brought to Mind Another Swedish Death Cleaning Insight

It's okay to admit that what you wanted at twenty, thirty, or forty doesn't always fit who you are at fifty, sixty, or beyond. And by tossing out what's not serving you now, you make room for new experiences—the good stuff that resonates with who you are at your core.

Next up, I reached behind my winter coats and discovered an unexpected jackpot: some old paintings that might actually be worth something. I made a note on my phone to write this artwork into my will, to be given to my son when I pass.

Plus I found more will-worthy items: the coin and stamp collection I started with my dad. Plus a pile of vintage *Mad* magazines. These had more than mere sentimental value but actual monetary value too.

So This Brought Me to Another Swedish Death Cleaning Epiphany

It's important to write your will and living will. Getting these documents in order ensures that whatever treasures you've got, both valuable and sentimental, find their way into the right hands and are not tossed aside or fought over.

Writing a will is the ultimate act of kindness. It prevents squabbles over your collection of vintage comics or who gets your grandma's teapot. It lets your loved ones focus on the good times with you and your epic jokes, rather than arguing over who gets what.

When you spell out your last wishes in a legal document, you also get to call the shots on your funeral. You can specify whether you prefer cremation or burial. The tone of your memorial, the music that should be played. Want a comedy roast instead of a somber wake? Or maybe you want everyone to wear bright colors instead of black? It's all about making sure your final act is on your terms, reflecting who you really were.

Plus, getting your end-of-life paperwork in order isn't just about making things easier for everyone else. It's also a powerful death reminder to yourself—to make the most out of every moment.

Because as I keep reminding you in this book:

In the grand scheme of things, we're all just temporarily not dead yet.

So I made a quick note in my phone to hire a lawyer for my wills. Plus, I created an End of Life Planner, where I detail where to find my will, passwords, and final wishes.

(Note: I thought the planner was so helpful, that I'm sharing it for FREE on my site. I titled it "Over My Dead Body" because it's for your loved ones to find when you're gone. Because love means not wanting your family to spend their grief arguing over who gets your ironic coffee mugs. Or guessing whether you'd prefer your ashes scattered over the Pacific or turned into a decorative paperweight. Grab it at notsalmon.com)

Next up I continued my death cleaning process.

I dug further into my closets and found a huge juicer—one of those beasts that could juice a sofa if you gave it enough time. When I bought it I imagined starting each day with fresh juice. But it simply turned into a $900 paperweight.

Looking at this juicer got me thinking about all the expensive, shiny things I've bought in a flurry of aspiration: the foot massager, the fancy Fitbit watch, the designer jewelry, the overpriced lipstick.

Maybe you relate, but for you it's that expensive car. Or expensive anything. We spend our lives collecting these talismans, believing each purchase brings us closer to becoming a more ideal version of ourselves.

We're creatures seduced by the shine, forgetting that "shine" is just another word for "distraction." As a result . . . many of us fall into the trap of measuring our success with the yardstick of possessions. And so we're all busy accumulating things. It's kinda absurd, but who am I to judge? I've bought my fair share of magic beans.

Yep, we humans have a thing for things. We're all spending like we're starring in our own little reality show called *Who Can Die with the Most Toys?* Why do we do it? Maybe it's because every shiny new gadget or fancy pair of shoes is like a little trophy. "Look at me, I'm successful, I can afford this ridiculously overpriced thing that does exactly the same thing as the cheaper version."

Our society, driven by consumerism, is constantly selling us the idea that the next big purchase will finally make us happy and self-confident. But guess what? That's a load of crap. Because once you've made that purchase, you're no longer on the shopper's high.

Here's the funny thing that Swedish death cleaning makes clear: When you look back at your life, you'll remember the joy of your vacation, not the pricey luggage you took with you.

And that's the crux of it.

We clutter our lives with things . . . when what really sticks are the moments, the unbuyable, untouchable memories that live in our laugh lines, not in the leather lines of a luxury couch.

Society has us hoodwinked. We're so busy chasing the dream, we forget to live. We're stuck in a perpetual loop of longing, accumulating, and longing again, failing to realize that it's experiences, not things, that bring real, lasting joy.

Life's greatest pleasures are intangible:

- The feelings of warmth from a shared laugh
- The rush of adrenaline from a daring adventure
- The fuzzy nostalgia of a familiar tune

Now, let's bring it back to the real purpose of this book: to remind you how to live your best life—by embracing core values that empower you to become your highest-potential self.

HOW DO POSSESSIONS FIGURE INTO THIS?

Short answer: They don't. Or at least, they shouldn't too much.

Now, I'm not advocating for you to become a nomad with no earthly possessions. Go ahead, enjoy yourself. Life should have indulgences. Even Aristotle explained that we humans are sensory creatures, and so our souls need delight. But—and here's the catch that Aristotle threw in—he was big on moderation.

So I suggest you shift your focus a little bit.

- Do less collecting and more connecting.
- Accumulate fewer things and more stories.

Because when you're on your deathbed and the final tally comes, you won't be counting your gadgets. You'll be remembering the day at the beach when the tide stole your shoes. Or the road trip with the wrong turns that led to the right diner, with a waitress who called everyone "darling" and gave out advice like candy.

What I'm saying is: Don't be seduced by the things you can touch.

True wealth isn't found in the heft of your bank account but the weight of the moments in your memory bank. So invest in misadventures, in belly laughs, in human connections. These are the true blue-chip stocks.

I'll tell you—no one on their deathbed has ever said, "I wish I'd bought the deluxe model." Nope. They think about the time they accidentally set the kitchen on fire trying to make dinner and ended up eating cold sandwiches in the backyard.

So, for the love of all that is good in this world—stop worrying about whether your phone is the latest model. Or if your car is the shiniest on the block.

If you're on board for prioritizing a life rich in experiences—rather than possessions—here are some tools to rethink your spending habits.

Invest in the intangible. Next time you feel the urge to upgrade something, consider upgrading your love relationship or an old friendship. Those are the investments that yield the richest returns. Trust me, the ROI on shared human experiences far outstrips anything with a price tag.

Buy what can't be boxed. Whenever you're about to buy something with a comma in the price tag, hit pause and think, "Could I use this money for an experience?" Maybe it's a weekend getaway or tickets to a concert. Whatever the alternative, make it something that contributes to your bank account of cherished memories. Start shifting your spotlight from "the next must-have" to the next "must experience."

Take matters into your own hands. If you're tempted to buy something pricey, ask yourself if there's a less expensive way to get what you really want. For example, instead of buying that lavish coffee maker, can you simply learn to make a better tasting cup of coffee with what you already own? If so, donate the money you were about to spend to your favorite charity instead. Or park it in an interest-earning savings account.

See through the lie of retail therapy. Stop treating stores like they're therapeutic institutions. When you need soothing, spend less time in the mall and more time in the moment, watching sunsets or faces in love or children playing in the spray of a broken fire hydrant. Collect sights, not stuff. You can't hang a moment in your closet, but you can keep making more of them—endlessly—simply by noticing life more. Your heart and spirit are the finest and most delicate instruments you'll ever have, capable of storing gigabytes of giggles and terabytes of love.

Be a winner. Still tempted to go on a shopping spree? Imagine this: You're on a game show, but instead of winning prizes, you win moments. The grand prize? A life so rich with experiences that your heart is bursting. Sounds better than any shopping spree, right? Well, guess what, you're on that game show—right now!

To sum it up: Good stories are the true currency of your existence. Best of all, they appreciate over time, getting funnier and better. No one ever walked away from someone who was sharing a good story and thought, "That was cool, but I wish they talked about their Rolex more."

So let's stop this spending-money madness, because it's not just about saving your money, it's about saving your soul from becoming as plastic and manufactured as the things you're tempted to buy.

All of this brings me to my very last Swedish death cleaning insight:

At the end of it all, you can't take a sports car with you, but a good story? That you can take anywhere, even into the next life, if there is one. And I bet it's a great conversation starter with the afterlife crowd.

17

COULDA, WOULDA, SHOULDA, SHUTTUPPA

> This chapter is about small, medium, and large regrets. If you have endured a huge trauma or crisis, you might need more support. We'll tackle such greater-sized struggles in a later chapter.

Ah, the coulda, woulda, shoulda regrets of life. Your personal trio of hecklers, jeering you on with every misstep and misfire.

I personally have a laundry list of regrets like these . . . longer than a CVS receipt.

Here's a snippet:

- I shoulda started saving and investing when I was in my twenties.
- I coulda let go of those toxic relationships sooner.
- I woulda written my screenplay before I became a busy mom.
- I shoulda spent more time with my grandma before she passed.

And the list goes on . . .

On a particularly curmudgeonly day, I imagine that there's an alternate universe out there with a better, wiser version of me who managed to avoid my regrets. And right now Alternate Universe Me is happily sipping champagne on a yacht. Or at least enjoying coffee without spilling it on her shirt.

Meanwhile, here I am, often feeling like many of my life choices were randomly made by a roulette wheel.

Of course, I also recognize it's foolish to wallow. Each moment spent regretting my past is a moment stolen from my present.

You know those times when you're driving, and you suddenly realize you don't remember steering for those last few miles? Life can be like that. If you're lost in thoughts about old regrets . . . you'll miss the live broadcast of your life happening right now. So you must put down your regrets and focus on the road before you. That's where your future lies. You can fill it with all sorts of wonderful possibilities. And even with new mistakes—some that are worth making—so you can learn and grow from them.

Let's be real here: Everyone screws up.

You're not special in your failings. But you can *become* special if you learn how to respond wisely to your failings—and take control of what you can influence. Like:

- Your attitude
- Your effort
- Your honesty with yourself

These are all in your domain. So focus on these things like a laser.

In a way, staying stuck in regrets is like refusing to turn the page on a novel that you're reading because you didn't like the last chapter—ignoring the fact that the resolution, the climax, the part where everything starts to makes sense, is yet to come.

You must view your life with *kindsight*.

Stop beating yourself up about your past.

Stop slapping your forehead and asking, "What was I thinking?"

Instead, breathe and ask the far kinder question, "What am I learning?"

Life is about progress—not perfection.

Forgive yourself and move on. You did your best at the time, for what you knew at the time, for who you were at that time. Your past is meant to learn from—not to live in. It's time to stop harming yourself with thoughts about your past!

If right now you're thinking, "Easier said than done," no worries! I'm about to give you tools to *get* it done.

THREE TOOLS FOR NIPPING REGRETS

In chapter 11, we talked about those huge, depressing, end-of-life regrets—the kind of regrets that hit people like a freight train right before they die. You know, the usual suspects: "I should've spent more time with my kids," or, "Why didn't I chase my dreams instead of rewatching *Breaking Bad* for the third time?"

Guess what? Your present, smaller coulda, woulda, shoulda regrets can eventually become tomorrow's big, existential, I-screwed-up-my-entire-life regrets . . . unless you nip them in the bud . . . *now*.

And that's exactly what we're gonna do in this chapter. We're going after those bite-sized regrets . . . and we're nipping them before they snowball.

So let's get nipping!

Tool 1: "I Am and So I Do" Statements

First things first: Let's replace those troublemaking "coulda, woulda, shouldas" with some helpful "I am and so I do" core-value-fueled statements.

I'll demonstrate with an example from my own life.

Let's say I want to reduce this grumbling regret:

I shoulda written a screenplay before I became a busy mom.

I ask myself these two questions:
- Who do I need to become to write that screenplay now?
- Who do I need to become to make sure I don't repeat this same type of regret in other areas of my life?

Next, I brainstorm some core values needed to move forward and become that person:

- Disciplined
- Determined
- Brave

I choose one single core value to work on.

In this case, I chose determination.

I then link this core value to a helpful habit and create an "I am and so I do" statement for my To-Die List.

- **I Am:** Determined.
- **I Do:** And so I write my screenplay for sixty minutes every day at 6 A.M.
- Boom. It's on my To-Die List.

Next, I schedule this "I am and so I do" statement in my Google Calendar—so I really (really) (REALLY) do it!

Basically, this "I am and so I do" statement becomes a stop and swap tool.

- First you stop your annoying "coulda, woulda, shouldas."
- Then you swap in a proactive "I am and so I do" thought-and-action step.
- You must do both: stop and swap!

Admittedly, not all regrets can be reshaped into to-do items, because some are set in the concrete of the past.

For example, consider this immovable regret of mine:

I coulda spent more time with my grandma before she passed when I was twelve years old.

Ouch. That's a painful thought. This regret has been lodged in my heart since I was a tween. I recognize that dwelling on this pain from my childhood won't bring back this person. And so, this regret can't become an action item to change the situation—because it's unchangeable.

So I ask myself this question:

Who do I need to become to make sure I don't repeat this same type of regret in other areas of my life?

I ponder, brainstorm, and realize:

When I was twelve my priorities were elsewhere. Friends seemed more pressing than the quiet company of my grandmother. When illness made my aging grandmother fragile, it frightened me. Love felt heavy. It had the weight of grief. Now, as an adult, I see things differently. Love isn't just a feeling. It's an action. It requires showing up, being present, and making sure that my actions reflect my love—that I'm not just passively feeling love but actively demonstrating it. Because nobody lasts forever.

And so from my childhood regret about my grandmother I glean the following lessons:

- Real love needs not only to be felt—but demonstrated.
- If I don't want this regret to happen again, I need to show my love out loud and in person—right there in the thorny, messy middle of life.
- Although I can't change the past, I can rewrite the future going forward.

Next, I brainstorm the core value I need to embrace to prevent this regret from reappearing. And "empathic love" pops out at me.

I then link this core value to a habit and write down the following:

I Am: Empathically loving.

I Do: And so I plan regular meet-ups with my loved ones—paying special mindful attention to anybody who is older or dealing with health issues.

Next, I make a physical list of people I love and schedule time to actually call them or visit regularly, writing my "I am and so I do" statement directly on my Google Calendar.

Basically, I create a pivot from dwelling on past mistakes to doing higher-level actions.

You can also apply this "pivoting tool" to daily small regrets.

For example . . . If you realize that you coulda, woulda, shoulda stood up better for yourself in an argument or a business meeting . . . you might brainstorm the following.

I Am: Assertive, confident, brave (pick one).

I Do: And so I bravely share my views in an assertive and respectful way.

You don't have to schedule all of these "I am and so I do" life lessons.

Some can serve as mantras to marinate your mindset with. If this is the case, just write them on Post-it notes and put them where you can read them often.

Or simply use your chosen core value as a "cue word"—a quick mental poke. Say your core value word out loud, or silently to yourself, and gently lure yourself into taking action as the ideal person you want to become.

Remember: Every blunder, every stumble, every faux pas isn't meant to be a quicksand pit of regret. It's meant to be a lesson to learn from. You cannot change the past for the better. But your past can change you for the better.

Admittedly, regret can be a very loud guest in the quiet house of your mind. And it can be an annoying guest too. One that refuses to leave. Even when you ask it politely.

At a certain point you need to tell this coulda, woulda, shoulda squatter ... to shuttuppa.

I know shuttuppa is a bit harsh. So I came up with two assertive and classy-worded ways to shush your regrets. This brings me to our next tools.

I recommend you use the words "forward" and "next" as mental reset buttons.

Tool 2: Forward

"Forward" is a very effective mantra to use when you're tempted to infinitely autopsy a dead relationship or life misstep of any kind. It's a great word to chant when love sours beyond repair, or when failure seems to be not just a moment but a monument.

Forward is your way of acknowledging that, yes, you coulda made a different choice. But here you are now, shoelaces tied, ready to move forward on a road that doesn't end at the scene of your stumble.

So next time your past starts calling, just tell it, "Forward!" Then focus your thoughts and actions in this forward direction.

Bonus Tip: Sometimes when I catch myself obsessing about a regret I pause and ask myself:

- Is this thought moving me forward to become Aspirational Eulogy Me?
- Or is this thought moving me backward to become a Bitter, Negative, Stuck Me?

- If it's backward, I vilify this regret and label it as a "Backward Thought." Then I tell myself, "Forward," and re-aim myself in that better forward direction.

Tool 3: Next

I want you to use this sharp little word, "Next," like a karate chop, to cut yourself free from the past's persistent cling. Tell yourself, "Next," whenever you find yourself dwelling on depressing regrets.

This word "Next" helps you to acknowledge there's always another chance, another door—another, more positive use of your mental energy.

Bonus Tip: I love to say, "Next," in a funny voice—like I'm some guy who works at a delicatessen counter, and I'm yelling out, "Neeeeeexxxxt"—because I'm ready to serve up something new.

For those of you who love a good metaphor (raising my own hand):

Think of "Forward" and "Next" as the sounds of you turning the page—and deciding that the narrative arc of your life is still ascending.

Imagine how you'll feel on your deathbed, when that string of coulda, woulda, shoulda regrets try to make their grand entrance—and they find the room already full with inspiring tales of how you pressed "Forward" and embraced "Next"—and how these words helped you to move on and build new things to celebrate.

Next and Forward will have turned out to be the best allies in your life—bringing out the stories that matter, the ones where you didn't stay stuck—you directed the traffic.

Sure, you might not have avoided those falls. But you found a way to rise from them. Again and again. Proving that what matters isn't how often you stumble, but that you *always* get up.

And THIS will be your legacy!

Not the perfection of a life without error! But the beauty of a life bravely lived!

As the final credits roll on your life, you'll even likely conclude that the best scenes were those where you overcame your regrets! You'll fondly recall those times you bravely stepped away from failed relationships, botched jobs, or misguided decisions that seemed, at one point, impossible to overcome.

You'll smile, thinking of your *resilience, discipline, confidence* . . . and each of the various core values you focused on. You'll take pride in knowing how these core values helped you to walk into the unknown, without those chains from the past weighing you down.

From this vantage point, your slip-ups won't feel like regrets. They'll feel like badges of honor . . . testaments to a life well lived.

So put down that burden of coulda, woulda, shoulda. You'll need your hands free to applaud when you finally take that bow on a life well lived.

18

GOT SOUL? WHO EXACTLY IS YOUR INNER YOU?

If you were to ask me to share my views about the soul, I'd respond, "How much time do you have?" Not because I have the answers, but because I know how this conversation goes. Down a never-ending rabbit hole.

The soul is an elusive concept, like mercury spilled from a thermometer—impossible to pin down.

Sure, we toss around the word "soul" with casual abandon. We say a song has soul. Or that a meal was soul-satisfying. We describe cities as soulless. But we never clearly explain the what and the how of the soul.

And so for eons, the nature of the human soul has been debated all over the place—in religious texts, philosophical essays, and late-night, booze-fueled conversations.

Theories on the soul vary . . .

It's the pilot light that won't go out . . . the eternal, unchanging essence of a person . . . your spiritual fingerprint.

Then there's the more cynical take . . .

It's a fanciful creation of the human mind—and we're all just complex networks of neurons firing.

I've thought about the soul many times in my life. Once during a dental procedure, under a too-bright light, with my oral surgeon hovering over me suggesting, "Count backward from ten." And there, between ten and the haziness of eight, I wondered if what made "me" a "me" was something more than my assembly of parts. I remember feeling like I was nearing an epiphany, right before I passed out. Apparently my version of an ayahuasca journey involves anesthesia and a surgical light.

So in the end, I'm as much in the dark about the soul as everyone else.

With this in mind, I thought we'd explore this metaphysical conundrum together . . . go down that rabbit hole—and see where we end up.

You go first!

I want YOU to think about what YOU feel in YOUR gut about the soul.

Why? Because your perception of your soul (or the lack thereof) will wind up deeply influencing how you choose to live your life—as well as how you choose to think about your inevitable death.

Take a minute to reflect:

- Does your soul exist? Does it kick back inside of you, experiencing life's highs and lows? At the end of your life, does your soul live on—and on—and on?

- Or do you believe that the idea of a soul is just a comforting idea we humans came up with—and in reality we're incredibly sophisticated bio-brain machines? So when the lights go out . . . that's it.

Ponder away. No rush. I'll wait.

Done? Great.

Which team are you on? "Team Soul Exists" or "Team Soul Skeptic"?

IF YOU'RE ON TEAM SOUL EXISTS

If you're boarding this soul train . . . then you feel you're more than just a transient, biological blip. You're a spark that refuses to be snuffed. You feel that your life and actions have a deeper, more lasting impact, because they will ripple through eternity.

Now, you've heard me promote the joy of ripples in chapter 12—explaining how our actions affect others, who then affect others, like the world's longest line of falling dominoes. But if you're on Team Soul, then these ripples travel even further. You carry them forward into future incarnations—like a kind of karmic carry-on bag. So every good deed, every blunder, every moment of kindness or spite—it's all stored within you, moving with you to the next soul train stop, with the hope that eventually you'll sort it all out.

Who's Riding This Soul Train with You?

Some pretty notable people, like ...

Aristotle: Yes, my favorite Greek philosopher believed in the soul. He wrote about how the soul is what gives life to the physical body, making it more than just a pile of parts. He also believed that the reason we're here on this planet is for the education of the soul.

Dr. Brian Weiss: The author of *Many Lives, Many Masters* also champions the soul. He views us humans as spiritual beings, living multiple lives, trying to level up our souls. According to Weiss, your present life's purpose is "soul correction." You've got lessons to learn, mistakes to mend, and growth to achieve. Those challenges you're facing? They're your soul's overdue homework from a past life. It's the universe's way of saying, "Let's keep working on that project called You."

Plus some of our world's brainiest folks in lab coats also believe in the soul.

John Eccles: He's a Nobel Prize–winning neurophysiologist. He believed that there's a divine aspect to human consciousness—and so we might have souls.

Arthur Eddington: He's an astrophysicist who believed that the meticulous order and beauty of the cosmos hinted at a spiritual realm and the possibility of souls.

Georges Lemaître: He's the big brain behind the Big Bang theory. He believed that our cosmos was a link to the divine and thereby, yes, it was possible we have souls.

Most religions preach about the soul too.

Christianity sees the soul as an eternal being, which is on a mission to hustle back to Heaven, by choosing to live by Jesus's playbook—practicing soul correction through repentance, forgiveness, love, and service.

Hinduism casts the soul as Atman, your true self, beyond ego and mind. Your life right now is your soul's school—with each reincarnation a chance to resolve karma and move closer to *moksha* (liberation from the cycle of birth and death).

Judaism breaks the soul down into parts—*nefesh, ruach, neshama*—each grappling with life's moral puzzles. The main underlying tenet: Your choices and ethical dilemmas are all a training ground for your soul.

So we've got philosophers, scientists, and religions on Team Soul. But that's not all. We've also got ...

Near-death experiencers (NDE-ers): These are the wild-card entrants in this soul debate—accidental tourists of the afterlife. NDE-ers speak of glowing lights and inner peace and a soul reunion with long-gone loved ones—a meetup of our soul with an eternal community of other souls.

What It Means If You Believe You Have a Soul

If you believe you have a soul, then every day is a test, a chance to learn something new, to become a better version of you. Every act of kindness, every leap of courage, every act of high-level virtue isn't just good behavior—it's an investment in your soul's overall portfolio.

Plus vice versa for your vices. The more bad you do in this life, the tougher your go-around might be in the next incarnation.

This perspective can feel like a burden at times. It's a lot of pressure, knowing your actions ripple through the cosmic accounting system. But it's also strangely exhilarating.

However . . . admittedly . . . not everybody reading this book is on Team Soul Exists—and that's okay! Perhaps you are one of the many soul skeptics.

IF YOU'RE ON TEAM CONSCIOUSNESS, ALSO KNOWN AS TEAM CORE SELF

If you're a soul skeptic, this means that you most likely believe that your "inner you" is not based in anything spiritual or mystical—but is the result of neurons firing and wiring, creating a "consciousness" or a "core self."

This soul-free belief has its perks. It frees you from worries of a judgmental afterlife. However, just because this viewpoint is soul free does not mean it's core-value free! If you're a champion of consciousness, then you probably still place a high premium on ethics. You understand that, even without spiritual brownie points on the line, living honorably is still important.

Who's on Team Conscious Core Self with You?

Again . . . you're in good company.

Martin Seligman: He's been dubbed the father of positive psychology and prefers terms like "mind," "consciousness," and "self" over the more mystical word "soul." He believes that living a life aligned with high-level core values leads the "self" to experience true fulfillment and flourishing.

Steven Pinker: This revered, sharp-minded psychologist believes our brains are running the show. And that our consciousness is like a complex brain software program. Forget ethereal entities. Our joys, sorrows, and moral dilemmas are all elegantly scripted by neural circuits.

Richard Dawkins: He's the famed evolutionary biologist who sees the idea of a "soul" as just mythic, poetic talk. He believes our feelings and moral compass are all thanks to natural selection.

Buddhism: According to Buddha's teachings, you don't have an eternal soul! Plus everything that you consider your "you"—your thoughts, feelings, love for mocha, dread of Mondays —is as fleeting as a Snapchat message. Clinging to the idea of any fixed concept of "self" (or eternal soul) is not just painful, it's as senseless as trying to catch smoke with your bare hands.

What It Means to Your Life If You Don't Believe in the Soul

If you believe only in the conscious self, you are free from those pesky long-term eternal repercussions. There is no cosmic ledger, no tallying of spiritual debits and credits. There is only this life, this moment. And there is a certain purity in that. A clarity that comes from knowing you have one act only.

Your choices become more important, precisely because they are finite.

This is your one shot at life. No encores, no sequels. So you ought to make your life a goodie, by living in a way you can feel proud about.

As a believer in a soul-free consciousness, you should still feel enthused to behave at your best. Not because it will balance out your spiritual books. But because it will make the here and now feel better, fuller, richer.

Guess what? Research actually supports this view too.

Studies show that "lower-level ethics" boomerang back to us with lower levels of happiness. It's a bit like eating cookie dough straight from the tube. Sure, it's fun in the moment. However, you're going to feel pretty terrible later.

Numerous studies support: The better your ethics, the better your life.

- Anita E. Kelly from the University of Notre Dame found that honest folks enjoy better mental and physical health than their more . . . creative, truth-bending counterparts.
- Sonja Lyubomirsky's studies reveal that chronic negative behaviors (letting your inner Darth Vader take the wheel) lead to greater dissatisfaction with life.
- Stanford research shows that hostile behavior isn't just emotionally toxic—it's physically toxic too, increasing your risk of heart disease. Being a jerk is, quite literally, bad for your heart.

And then there's the wisdom of hindsight. Cornell University research highlights a major regret among the elderly: not being kinder or more ethical in their lives. Nobody on their deathbed says, "I wish I'd been a bigger jerk to people." It's always, "I wish I'd spent more time with loved ones," or, "I should have done more to help others."

So even if you are a soul skeptic who believes in a Core Self Limited-Edition Singular Life, you will still get rewarded for your good behavior—in the very life you're living right now. Basically, love and kindness are not means to an end, but the very ends in themselves.

Your core self knows: When you reach the finish line, you'll want to leave behind a legacy that's a little less *Here lies a grade-A douchebag* . . . and a little more *Here stands a decent human being*.

SOUL OR NO SOUL?

So, what happens if you find it hard to pick a side in the "Is My Soul Real . . . or Have I Just Had Too Much Coffee?" debate?

I know how that feels. Personally, I'm sort of split. I like the idea of a soul. I mean, who wouldn't want to be more than a brief flicker in the vast cosmos? Yet the skeptic in me clings to the tangible. As a result, I'm always thumbing through research studies to figure things out further, like a detective at the scene of a metaphysical mystery.

At this point I've coined myself as "spirituallogical." I'm a hybrid creature with one foot in the metaphysical waters and the other on the solid ground of science.

I'm not full-on "woo-woo." I'm more of a single "woo."

Maybe you are too. And because we wander back and forth between believing in the mysteries of the soul versus the intricacies of the human brain, we can see how much both viewpoints share in common.

The big irony: In the end, it doesn't matter if you're on Team Soul or Team Core Self.

What matters is that you play the game of life with solid core values. Because those are your true scorecards, no matter which team you're playing on.

- If you believe in the soul, then you'll want to pursue *soul* correction and evolve in this *lifetime*.
- If you believe in a core self, you'll want to pursue *core self* correction and grow who you are in this *life*.

So, whether you believe you've got a soul under the hood ... or just a supercharged consciousness ... what really matters is that you try to learn lessons from your stumbles and keep moving forward, aimed at becoming Aspirational You.

In order to do this, you must acknowledge that you have a YOU inside of you.

It doesn't matter what you call this YOU—just know it's always with you.

Give a Little Nod to This YOU Right Now

Because, frankly, this YOU is significant. It's a unique, irreplaceable, one-of-a-kind YOU. Treat it as such.

This is the YOU inside you who has been busy reading these words this whole time, pondering whether you have a soul or core self. And this YOU needs to be brought in more regularly for more mindful and soulful consultations.

You get to pick the adjective, "mindful" versus "soulful." Just make sure you're picking your YOU to run your life. Give this YOU a soapbox and microphone and design a life based on what matters most to this YOU.

- NOT to your parents.
- NOT to your overly opinionated uncle.
- NOT to coworkers who wear burnout like a medal.
- NOT to your ex who thought dreaming big was dreaming too much.
- NOT to glossy magazines, billboards, and TV commercials that like to scream, "Be like this! Look like this!"
- NOT to those hovering chaperones of doubt and self-consciousness who are always telling the Fun You to pipe down . . . and the Sad You to pretend to cheer up.
- NOT to those Lures of Comparison that like to dim your uniqueness . . . then stuff it into a box marked "normal."
- NOT to the crushing, cruel weight of fear—which makes you feel smaller, makes you say yes when you mean no, and makes you swallow your wild, wonderful goals for life.

You must recognize each of these entities for the paper tigers they are. And you must walk right through them—as weird, wonderful YOU—into a story of your own making!

You Must Be the YOU Who TRULY Feels Like YOU

- The YOU who loves weird documentaries and eats pickles straight from the jar
- The YOU who gets misty-eyed over beautiful old buildings
- The YOU who enjoys spending Saturday nights mastering the art of making the perfect omelet
- The YOU who dreams in vivid colors about building a tree house in your backyard . . . or taking a cruise on the Caribbean

Know this now: The YOU-ier you are—the happier you will be.

If you want to create a life you truly love, you must align your actions with your YOU's deepest core values—and do whatever Soul Correction or Core Self Correction is needed—so you can leave behind a legacy you're proud of.

Plus, you must march to the rhythm of that little drummer in your gut.

- Read more books that make you miss your subway stop.
- Listen to more songs that make you turn up the car radio.
- Hang out with more people who get your jokes—and not only understand your quirks but celebrate them.
- Be proud of whatever makes you weird . . . because that's your YOU's light shining through. Never dim your YOU's light for anyone . . . even if others make you feel bad that it's shining too brightly in their eyes. In fact, be sure to shine your YOU's light as brightly as possible . . . so other awesome weirdos from your tribe can be sure to find you.

WHAT'S THE TAKEAWAY?

In the end, when you're tallying up your life's greatest hits . . . it will be a list of those times when you were truest to your YOU. So it doesn't matter what team you're on, Soul or Synapse. A life well lived is all about whether you're listening to the team captain . . . and that captain is your inner YOU.

You need to give this YOU the floor. Because whether it's a soul or a circuit doing the talking, what it has to tell you will help you to create the most fulfilling blueprint for your life.

What's stopping you from listening to this YOU?

Distractions galore. A lot of noise—posing as important. Yes, life is full of flashing lights and alarms, like a casino floor designed to make you lose track of time, money, and yourself. The strange part is: Most of the distractions don't even pretend to be meaningful. They're just there, insistent, a thousand tiny "Look at me!" moments in the daily parade of nonsense.

And you, like everyone else, gets easily pulled along, scrolling, clicking, and spending whole days on things you won't remember tomorrow.

So coming up in the next chapter, I'll show you how to pull your focus out of all that noise . . . and wrangle back a little quiet . . . enough to hear what the real you has to say.

19

ARE YOU HAVING A NEAR-LIFE EXPERIENCE?

Remember those days when we used to pay attention to things that weren't on a screen? Yeah, me neither.

If you're like me, there are many days that your thumbs do more walking than your feet. You scroll, tap, and swipe . . . and get a lot done, right from the confines of your home.

The result? Far too often you . . .

- Text . . . instead of enjoying a deep talk in person.
- Order a rideshare . . . instead of taking a nice, leisurely walk.
- Listen to a podcast . . . instead of listening to your inner voice's opinions.
- Pursue "likes" in social media . . . instead of sitting with the people you like.

The other day, I saw someone drop their phone on the sidewalk, and the look on their face was the same as if they'd accidentally let go of a baby. We've become so tethered to our devices that I invented a term for what this is doing to our lives:

Near-life experiences.

If you read this book's introduction (and gold star if you did), you've already heard me rant about this topic. Near-life experiences occur when you're physically present but mentally checked out, lost in some pixelated purgatory, spellbound by your screen or some other distraction. So you're surrounded by life, but not in it. You're just life adjacent.

Unfortunately, near-life experiences can become daily occurrences.

- You sit across from your friends, only half listening to what they're saying, because your phone just vibrated.
- You're on a beautiful hike, and you spend so much time taking photos of trees . . . that you actually walk into one.
- You're at a party, but instead of talking to people, you're just posting about it on social media.

These are just a few examples where you're there but you're not. You're almost connecting, almost living fully, almost embracing the rawness of existence. But then, nope, you gotta check that notification or take that photo.

Let's not mince words: If living a life true to yourself means anything to you, then you must have the cajones to put down your phone and look life in the eye.

Sure, real life can feel uncomfortable at times. But it's *real*. And isn't that the point? Those messy, imperfect, face-to-face interactions? Those are the ones that intimately connect your YOU to someone else's YOU. No amount of pixels can replicate the deep connection of shared in-person laughter!

Worst of all, these screens are not just screening you off from intimacy with others! They're also blocking you from intimacy with yourself. They're busying your thoughts with so much noise that you can't hear what your YOU is trying to tell you.

Meaning? If you want to live a life that's authentically yours, you must put down your phone and dedicate some time to quiet contemplation. Only in solitude do you get the space you need to think and grow.

For example, when you're in deep contemplation, you might suddenly realize . . .

Uh-oh! When I am in a fight with my partner, my ability to remember specific details is like a superpower. But instead of saving the world, it's ruining my relationship.

Basically, you need quiet contemplation in order to perk up and listen to what your inner YOU is saying. Because if you're not listening, you won't grow—you'll plateau.

You must prioritize screen-free time in solitude, because at the end of the day, and the end of everything . . .

- The relationship you have with yourself is the most important one you'll ever have.
- And the most important conversations you'll ever have will be the ones you have with yourself.

Unfortunately, if you're like most people . . . you now pay far more attention to your cell phone than your "soul phone." *

As a result, messages from your YOU are getting buried beneath phone notifications while you attend to the trivial and immediate.

Except here's the thing: Most of the time *you're not really busy.* That's a smokescreen. You're simply terrified to pick up your soul phone. After all, a lot of what it has to tell you is difficult to hear. Like how you're not always the hero of your story. Sometimes you're the villain or nincompoop.

You think, "I'll just deal with all of that stuff later."

Admittedly, it's easier to stay cocooned in a version of yourself that never has to evolve. But ignoring your soul phone's ring doesn't fix your issues. It just adds more layers between you and authentic YOU. Over time your authentic self becomes like an old friend you've ghosted . . . who you've grown far apart from.

In a way, your cell phone is a soul blocker.

Meaning? Every time you choose your cell phone over your soul phone, you block an opportunity for greater growth and higher happiness. So, next time your soul phone rings, don't ignore it. Bravely pick up, say hello to your inner YOU, and get ready to chat with the most insightful, most honest version of yourself.

Quick warning: The more you ignore the ringing of your soul phone, the louder and more frequently it will ring to get your attention—in the form of repeated patterns of pain, and eventually as "supersize me crisis pain."

---

* I use the word "soul" a lot, because of the playful wordplay. If you're on Team Core Self, simply do a stop and swap and mentally replace it with your preferred term.

The truth: Many of us are mired in huge amounts of emotional pain because we're not listening to the insights and wisdom of our inner YOU.

Writer Anaïs Nin said it well in her poem "Risk": "And the day came when the risk to remain tight in a bud was more painful than the risk it took to blossom."

Meaning? When you bravely listen to your inner YOU, you're taking the risk to bloom.

So, let's talk about *how to be more present in your own life.*

First off, you really need to get better at using your mobile phone in moderation. And yeah, I get it, that's like saying, "Hey, just eat the top layer of this triple-decker chocolate cake." It's very, very difficult.

Secondly, you also need to find ways to deal with all those other screens too—each one a little fortress that keeps the real world at arm's length.

Happily, I have four tools to empower you to start turning your attention away from technology, so you can better hear the messages being broadcast from your YOU.

Tool 1: Create a No-Phone Zone

I want you to put down your phone . . . back away from it slowly . . . then stay away for a few hours.

A few months ago I bravely went on a twelve-hour digital detox. I turned off my phone from 7 AM to 7 PM. It felt like a throwback Thursday to the 1990s.

I started my day sitting in a chair and reading a paper newspaper—like one of those historical reenactment villages, showing kids what life was like before we could swipe right.

Next, I made breakfast without snapping a photo of it. It tasted better than usual. Was I imagining that?

Then I took a walk outside, and I saw how people were completely entranced by their little glowing screens. Not noticing the sky, or the birds, or the faces of other human beings. I wanted to tell them what I'd just discovered, that the sky was particularly blue that day. But I realized that might make me sound crazy.

With my phone off, I noticed I could hear things more clearly.

The sounds of traffic. The wind. And my own thoughts, which were tentative at first, like a deer on a meadow at dawn, not quite sure if the coast was clear.

But then soon my thoughts began entering more confidently.
- I thought up new ideas for articles to write. Then had a realization: Ideas are not born in a vacuum. Ideas have parents and grandparents.
- I remembered an old photo of my mom and dad sitting on a camel.
- I began thinking about how my mom used to be taller than me. But now she's shorter, shrinking as she ages. I made a mental note: Call mom more . . . before the inches run out.
- I thought about how fear can be a symmetrical mirror image of desire. To fear losing something or someone is just another way of saying you love it fiercely.
- I remembered how my son mistakenly called the "Statue of Liberty" the "Statue of Delivery." I decided it was time to learn new recipes and stop ordering food so much.

When I came home from my walk, I felt proud of how I was living tech free. However, as evening crept in, the phone withdrawal started to hit. My eyes began to crave something speedier to look at than the slow-paced real world. I felt this pang, like maybe I was missing out on something. What if someone was desperately trying to reach me, to say something important—like how they'd just spotted Bigfoot?

When 7 PM finally hit, I turned on my phone—and was greeted with a digital avalanche. Messages, notifications, alerts . . . but no Bigfoot sightings. The world, it seemed, had survived quite well without me.

Yet something lingered. An imprint of the day's quiet, a sense that something lost had been briefly found. And so I decided to do digital detoxes once monthly.

I highly recommend you too create no-phone zones! If twelve hours seems too long, start smaller. Just commit to carving out a little pocket of non-doing in your world of constant doing.

- Thirty minutes of your morning, spared from the onslaught of emails
- Ten minutes walking outside, where your phone sees nothing but the inside of your pocket

Start making these small rebellions against the urgent. Silent refusals to be always available, always responsive. In these moments, you will meet yourself. The real you. Not the curated you, shaped and shined for public consumption. But the raw, unedited version of YOU. And I predict that this YOU will have some interesting things to tell you.

Tool 2: Write Makes Inner Might

If you want to be more present in your life, you need to get familiar with the uncharted territories of your mind. Not those everyday, surface-level thoughts. I mean the real stuff: the buried, inconvenient truths that love to hide behind your daily distractions.

So it's time to grab your journal again—and write the following prompt at the top of a blank page . . . then just stare at it . . . until your brain can't help but spill its guts.

What do I need to know that I don't want to know?

This is a journaling question for the brave, for those ready to poke the sleeping bear of their subconscious. Actually, it's more than just a question. It's an invitation to confront those squirming, awkward truths you'd rather not face.

- Maybe it's realizing that you need to walk away from someone or something.
- Maybe it's facing a fear . . . or finally admitting to a secret desire.
- Or maybe it's about recognizing that you've been treating your body more like a landfill than a temple.

Plus here are some other prompts . . . that help to make the unseen seen.

- What limiting beliefs did my childhood instill in me about love, or money?
- Which parts of me do I hide because I fear they are too much, or not enough?
- If I were immune to failure, what dream would I chase?

Make it a regular habit to journal about brave questions—about your wins, your flops, and your "why the heck did I do that?" moments. The more you get in the habit of showing up on the page, the more you'll be able to show up in your actual life.

Tool 3: Vow to Become a Better Noticer

The inspiring author Paulo Cuelho is known for saying: "You can become blind by seeing each day as a similar one. Each day is a different one, each day brings a miracle of its own. It's just a matter of paying attention to this miracle."

Cuelho's quote kinda reminds me of what Nobel Prize–winning scientist Daniel Kahneman said.

Kahneman believed that we all experience about 20,000 individual "moments" in a day. 20,000! That's a staggering amount. However, many of us miss most of them—because we're too busy stewing over the past or pre-gaming the future.

But, if you really want to kick up your life a notch, you must start noticing what's happening right in front of you.

You need to become a world-class "noticer" of small moments.
- The way someone's face shifts when they leave the gym—a mix of *"thank God"* relief that it's over . . . and *"damn, I did it"* pride
- The awkward gait of a dog wearing a sweater—trying to adapt its wolf ancestry to this newly acquired gig as a fashion model
- The hurried swiping of someone using a dating app in public—each left swipe a micro-breakup

Life is made of these tiny moments—some ridiculous, some sublime—but you've got to slow down long enough to catch them. Or they're gone.

Plus art and music? These are also important in your noticer's tool kit.

A big reason we love music and art? They're powerful at hijacking our wandering brains and dragging us straight into the here and now. When you're lost in a song or staring at a painting, you're fully absorbed in "now time."

And memories? Those are our scrapbook of *"now time"* moments.

Memories are what happen when you're so fully present that your brain says, "This matters. Don't delete it."

And those years that feel blurry, like they've been erased from the tape?

That's what happens when you're speeding through life on autopilot. And you weren't present enough to give your brain a reason to hit "save."

You've got this one life. And yes, it can be messy and baffling. But if you can train yourself to be a better noticer, you'll gather a mosaic of meaningful memories that will remind you: *Yes, I was here. I lived fully. I paid attention.*

Tool 4: Shut Up and Meditate

Imagine you're just chilling on your couch and a genie pops out and says, "Here's a magic potion that will give you incredible clarity about who you are and what you want for your life!"

Exciting, right? You'd guzzle that potion in one gulp. Well, guess what? There is such a thing—it's called meditation!

Regular meditation sharpens your mind, heightens self-awareness, and boosts emotional health. It's a chance to be fully present and just let your inner you get a word in edgewise. Think of it like hitting refresh on your brain's operating system—all while lounging on your couch doing, ostensibly, nothing.

Now, there are a thousand ways to meditate. Some people light candles or incense. Some like to chant, repeat mantras, or ring bells. But I like to keep it simple, because if meditation is going to work, it has to be *doable*.

So, I recommend you try a mindful breathing meditation—basic but effective.

1. Find a cozy spot in your home. It could just be a chair in your bedroom or a spot on your couch.
2. Sit comfortably, but don't get too comfortable. (We're aiming for awareness, not a nap.)
3. Close your eyes . . . or just soften your gaze. Whatever feels more natural.
4. Take a deep breath in through your nose . . . then let your breath out through your mouth. Pay attention to the sensations of your breath. The way the air feels as it enters your nose, fills your lungs, then leaves again through your lips.
5. Do this for a few minutes.

Now, at some point—and this happens every time—your mind is going to throw some weird stuff at you.

You might notice thoughts like:

- "Why did I agree to dinner with those people?"
- "How long is this going to take?"
- "Did I turn the stove off?"
- "Why does my ex keep showing up in my dreams?"

Don't fight those thoughts. Let them float by . . . like passing clouds . . . without any judgment.

Then gently guide your focus back to your breath. Breathing in through your nose . . . and out through your mouth. Rinse and repeat for five minutes.

Over time, try to work your way up to fifteen minutes of meditation. Think of these sessions as visits to yourself. Like going to see a friend in the hospital even when they say they feel fine and don't need visitors. You're just checking in . . . making sure everything really is fine.

If you're resistant to meditation, try adding it your To-Die List with the following "I am and so I do" core-value-based statement:

- **I am:** Authentically me.
- **I do:** And so I meditate daily to get clearer on my thoughts, priorities, and core values.

Give it a shot! A little regular meditation goes a long way toward helping you tune into that inner YOU—the one who actually knows what you want . . . and how to get it.

Bonus: Calming down your anxious brain can also help you figure out where your car keys are.

20

LOVE IN THE TIME OF EMOJIS: SEEKING EMOTIONAL DEPTH IN A BUSY WORLD

When you're on your deathbed, and you're tallying up your life like it's some kind of cosmic Yelp review, guess what's going to count the most to you? The love stuff.

I am not just talking about romantic love. I'm talking about the whole love shebang: the love for your friends, family, coworkers—and even that neighbor whose day you brighten just by remembering their dog's name.

Know this now: The quality of your life is pretty much defined by the quality of your relationships. If you really want to live well ... *you've got to love well*.

After all, we're social animals, built to connect. That's been true since we were doodling on cave walls, and it's still true in our era of smartphones. It hasn't changed.

What has changed is everything else: technology, pace of life, our priorities.

Unfortunately, in today's modern world, many of us are caught up with collecting a quantity of friends like baseball cards. Or compressing our feelings into emojis—and turning our conversations into rapid-fire texts.

Here's a splash of cold, harsh reality: That's a shoddy blueprint for meaningful connections.

If you truly crave fulfilling relationships, you gotta hit pause on your speedy existence and actually listen to people. I mean, *really* listen—so people feel seen, heard, and understood.

Do this consistently, and when the final curtain falls, you'll be able to say, "Yeah, I did alright."

However . . . if you don't do this, well . . . remember those "five regrets of the dying" that I shared in chapter 11? Three of those were related to relationships.

- "I wish I'd had the courage to express my feelings."
- "I wish I had stayed in touch with my friends."
- "I wish I hadn't worked so hard."

I don't want you to wind up with these deathbed regrets. So, let's do a quick little exercise now.

1. Turn to a blank page in your journal.
2. Write down the names of the people who mean the most to you. Those whose absence would make your life significantly less bright.
3. Got 'em? Good. Now, next to each name, jot down the last meaningful conversation you had with them. When was it? What was it about?
4. Next, consider: If you were to disappear tomorrow, what would you wish you had said to them and what gestures would you wish you had done for them?
5. Why the heck haven't you said and done this yet? What steps can you take right now to strengthen your bond with these people?

Remember, this exercise isn't about making you feel guilty. It's about giving you perspective . . . and a gentle nudge to improve your love connections.

Because at the end of it all, you're not going to be reminiscing about those endless Zoom meetings. No, you'll be appreciating the laughter that made you double over, the hugs that felt like they could squeeze the bad days out of you, and all those tiny gestures that said "I love you" without uttering a word.

With this in mind, in this chapter I'll be exploring how to improve your daily rituals of love—because these are the unsung heroes of a life well lived.

Scientific research backs me up on this.

Take the Harvard Study of Adult Development, for instance. This study tracked 268 people for over eighty years, and you know what they found? Good relationships keep us happier and healthier.

I know this sounds like a no-brainer, like being told to wear a coat when it's cold. But sometimes the obvious needs to be repeated lots of times for the weight of it to sink in.

Let this sink in:

Deep, quality relationships are not just the icing on the cake of life. They're the whole damn cake.

At the end of the day, your most valued relationships need to be a priority. Not an afterthought. Not something you only pay attention to when there's a problem. And your inner circle should be loving, safe-feeling, intimate.

Let me tell it to you straight: At your funeral, nobody's going to recite your bank balance or list your collected appliances. However, they will talk about the day you drove through a snowstorm to make it to their side during a challenging time. And they'll discuss the countless cups of coffee you shared while trying to untangle the knotted threads of their dilemmas. And they'll fondly recall the way your eyes twinkled when you laughed.

This will be your most treasured legacy—the love you gave, the connections you nurtured.

And so I recommend you double down on creating meaningful connections—by fully embracing these two key core values:

- Empathic love
- Authenticity

Coming up, I will help you to embrace a range of practices related to these core values.

But first up, let's dive into what each really means.

EMPATHIC LOVE

Empathy is the ingredient that takes a relationship from good to great, from "I love you" to "I understand you." It's the difference between a nod and a reach, between polite concern and the kind of love that makes you put your phone down during dinner.

And in today's world of one-click purchases and five-second attention spans, taking the time to genuinely listen and understand someone else's feelings is practically a radical act.

So it's no surprise that John Gottman, the relationship researcher who's spent his career watching how couples connect (or don't), found that the more "empathetic engagement" partners show each other, the longer their relationship lasts.

With this in mind, empathy deserves a top spot on your checklist for a good partner—right up there with a good sense of humor.

In the end, empathy is what makes love not just bearable ... but beautiful. Because it's easy to love someone in their moments of strength and joy. But to love them in their moments of vulnerability, to empathize with their struggles ... that's where true, fulfilling love is found.

Consider a Marriage Going Through the Symbolic Motions of Love but Devoid of Empathy

Gifts are given, kisses are exchanged, sweet nothings are whispered. Yet without empathy there's a disconnect. Over time, this kind of marriage becomes a shared space rather than a shared life.

Without empathy, every argument is just a shout into the void—with "You always!" and "You never!" being lobbed like grenades.

But with empathy, disagreements are less about winning the argument and more about trying to understand where the other person is coming from. (Plus empathy stops you from offering, "I'm sorry you feel that way" as a hollow apology.)

Now, empathy doesn't make things perfect. Oh no. It makes things more real. You still notice the other person's flaws, their quirks, their morning breath. But you love them anyway. Because empathy shows you why this real person is who they are.

Empathy Isn't Easy

You have to put in the effort to actively listen—*not just wait for your turn to talk.*

You have to be mindfully present—*and value someone else's perspective as deeply as your own.*

You have to be patient—*and let's be honest, sometimes after a long day, patience can be scarce.*

Empathy is not a switch you flip. It's more like a muscle you have to keep working out. And sometimes it gets sore.

But the beautiful thing about empathy is: *It grows stronger the more you use it.*

And the beautiful thing about life is: *It's never too late to start being more empathic.*

Next up . . . let's do a deep dive into that second core value.

AUTHENTICITY

Ever said, "fine," when you meant, "I'm actually kinda upset?" You gotta fix that and sync your inner monologue with your outer dialogue. If you want meaningful relationships, you need to dare to stand in the open, without your armor, stripped of pretenses, fully visible.

Think of it as emotional nudism.

Is it frightening? Sure. Necessary? Even more so.

Imagine you're at the end of your life, looking back.

Do you want to be thinking about all the things you didn't say—because you kept sharing polite but shallow exchanges and emotional white lies?

Or do you want to know that you put it all out there—that you lived your emotional life with the volume turned up?

Pause for a second.

- Think about your recent interactions.
- Were you authentically you?
- Or were you choosing to be someone else's idea of who you should be?

If it's the latter, it's time to express your real opinions, even when they aren't popular. Screw conformity. Be unapologetically yourself. Own your quirks and preferences. Start saying "no," recognizing it's not a dirty word. You don't need anyone's approval to be the magnificent weirdo that you are.

Of course, you must be selective about who you choose to be vulnerable with. But those important people—the ones you keep in your inner circle? Don't hold back with them! And don't let them hold back either. Push them to peel off their masks. Authenticity only works if it's mutual, a give-and-take of truths, where both sides honor the unspoken pact of genuine connection.

This usually happens best when two people are talking in person, not filtered through screens or stretched thin by texts. So do more face-to-face meet-ups. And make sure that this intimate time together truly feels intimate.

Don't fall into the habit of handing each other metaphorical glossy brochures of your lives. Or discussing things in bullet points: promotions, vacations, quiche recipes, meticulous details of home renovations.

Don't let social media trick you into presenting only your highlight reels. You don't need to edit out the messy bits that don't fit into a certain narrative you want to portray.

If you're not careful, it's easy to fall into the habit of sitting across from people in cute cafés that smell like burnt espresso and ambition, flipping through the rehearsed pages of your lives, following the prescribed formula: mention, nod, smile, sip, repeat.

Seek out the messiness of real connection, the stuff that doesn't make it into holiday cards or social media feeds.

When you're with the people you love, put in the time and effort to explore their unpolished truths. The fears. The failures. The second guesses. Talk about the situations you feel stuck in, the relationships that aren't what you expected, the quiet panic of achieving everything you thought you wanted . . . only to find it lacking.

These are the conversations that linger. The ones that stick to your ribs like comfort food.

The truth is: Intimacy is found when someone shares the bits of their lives that are frayed around the edges. When someone says, "Here's the messy part of me," and you say, "Same here."

I encourage you: Drop the act. Set aside the narrative of constant success and perpetual happiness. Share your defeats, your worries, your I'm-not-so-sures. Steer your conversations into deeper waters. You'll create a space for the other person to do the same. Together you'll bolster one another's courage to reveal the more complicated truths of your lives.

It's time to disrupt the script. Forget what's "safe to share." True connection comes from having the courage to admit what we fear to say aloud. It's what happens when the texture of your voice begins to break—because you're telling that story you swore you'd never tell—the one that makes you squirm a little. Suddenly, there's a bending of heads, the meeting of eyes. It becomes a tender choreography, this dance of daring dialogue. No one's stepping on toes anymore because no one's trying to lead. You're just moving together, gliding, waltzing with words.

When you listen deeply like this, really give yourself over to the sound of someone else's voice, their words begin to bloom. They sense the space you're holding open for them. And so they feel safe to let their sentences unfurl, stretch out, relax into the sunlight of your attention.

When you actively listen like this, you're not just hearing words. You're hearing what's between them.

- Hopes dressed up as jokes
- Fears masquerading as anecdotes

It's a bit like being a detective, only what you're solving isn't a crime—but the mystery of another human being. *And isn't that something?*

You start to wonder: Maybe this is what it's all about. Finding these moments of genuine authentic connection in the din of daily life. Maybe amid the endless chase for what's next, the true prize is the pause—the quiet space where we allow ourselves to truly see and be seen.

It's a kind of art, this active listening. And it's a kind of love too.

It's saying, "Your words aren't just passing through. They're taking root."

In a world that constantly feels like it's spinning too fast for us to get a good look at each other, listening actively to someone is no small thing. It's your silent war cry, saying, *Here I am, bucking the trend, turning my full beam of focus onto you, you fascinating, narrative-spinning creature you.*

Active listening is thereby not just a gift of time . . . but a gift of spirit too.

To listen—*really actively listen*—is to say, "I have nowhere else to be . . . but here . . . with you."

All of this applies to all relationships: friendships, work relationships, and yes, yes, yes, love relationships too!

It's easy to love someone when they're fresh from the shower, smelling like lavender and handing you a plate of pancakes. It's something else to love them when they're down with the flu, resembling a character from *The Walking Dead*, and they've just used the last of the toilet paper.

The point is: If you want an intimate, lasting relationship, you've got to accept your partner as the flawed, authentic human that they are.

True love is less about driving off into the sunset together—and more about being willing to help your partner push their car when it breaks down on the side of the road.

True love is ...
- Dealing with your partner when they're a stressed mess—*then learning to talk calmly when you'd rather scream.*
- Putting in the effort to look them in the eye during hard times—*when you'd rather turn away.*
- Trying find the humor in a heated debate over whether a towel can be deemed "dirty"—*if it has only been used to dry clean hands.*

Here's the deal: Every morning when you wake up next to your wife, husband, or long-term love partner, you have a choice to make.

- You can look at your partner and think, "What the hell have I done with my life?"
- Or you can say, "Hell, yeah. Let's do this."

Because staying married or together isn't a one-time choice. It's a daily decision. True love is about choosing each other, again and again. Even when the choice feels hard. And even when the world outside your door seems like it's filled with easier options.

Important disclaimer about marriage: Some relationships are truly dysfunctional. Love should never feel like you're the only one rowing a two-person boat, fighting the currents alone. If this is you, then it's okay to reconsider things. If you're stuck with someone who enjoys making waves more than sailing smoothly, who can't steer clear of being self-centered, abusive, dishonest, or just plain toxic . . . then it's okay to choose to sail solo. This isn't about giving up. It's about understanding that true commitment is rowing together, not drowning quietly by someone's side.

THE PRACTICE OF MEANINGFUL CONNECTION

If you want to ensure you're experiencing deep, fulfilling relationships—follow these six principles.

1. **Every day, make a conscious effort to nurture your inner circle connections.** Don't allow TV, social media, or work to become more important than the people you love. Remember, Dorothy from *The Wizard of Oz* never said, "There's no place like office."

2. **Hold your replies.** We're often so busy rehearsing our next line that we miss the play. Try this during your next conversation: Listen like there's going to be a quiz later. The prize? A richer, deeper relationship. Aim for dialogue over monologue.

3. **Dive deeper with curiosity:** Listening isn't just about catching words. It's about fishing for feelings, for the unspoken. Ask questions as if you're uncovering a mystery where every clue counts. After the conversation, let it linger like the aftertaste of a fine wine. Reflect on what you've learned, not just about the other person, but about yourself, too.

4. **Express more appreciation.** Everything we say about someone at funerals—you should be saying it to that person now.

5. **Don't let annoyances pile up until they become Godzilla-sized.** Speak up and seek understanding over victory. Imagine you and your loved ones as captains in a sport called "emotional honesty," and even when it's tough, you play to win together.

6. **Make kindness your default setting.** Choose words that feel like marshmallows: soft, gentle, and unlikely to cause injury. Every time you feel upset, embrace self-control. "Can you please clean the dishes?" beats, "Why does the living room look like we're auditioning for *Hoarders*?" Plus remember, it's not only what you say, but how you say it . . . preferably not at decibels that scare the dog.

Life Is Short—Make Your Love Huge

In the end, life is about the connections you make and the lives you touch. Knowing that life is short and you're on the clock makes the act of loving someone both more urgent and courageous.

It's as though the universe has double dared us: "Go ahead, love lots of temporary beings, throw your fragile heart into relationships that won't last forever, because no human does." And in our stubborn, magnificent folly, we say, "Fine. Challenge accepted." We love, knowing it will hurt. We love, knowing it will end. And in doing so, we thumb our noses at death and affirm our appreciation for this blessing of a life.

We're only here briefly. We're a blip on the universe's timeline.

So you might as well be a blip that burns brightly, right?

21

YOU'RE NEVER TOO OLD
TO REJIGGER YOUR LIFE

Did you ever notice that we spend the first half of our time on this planet being told we're too young for things? You're too young to cross the street, too young to stay up late, too young to watch this movie.

Then, one day, without any warning, you're suddenly too old. Too old for late-night parties, too old for sequined dresses, too old for skateboards.

Basically, there's like a ten-minute window in your thirties—somewhere between paying off student loans and your first colonoscopy—when society thinks you're just right. And if you blink, you miss it.

But here's the thing about this "you're too old" story.

It's all baloney.

There's no rule book that says, "After age sixty-three you're too old to wear leather pants, too old to dye your hair pink, too old to start a new hobby/skill set, too old to find new love."

We need to stop paying attention to this flimsy notion of being age appropriate. There's no cosmic referee who's going to blow a whistle and say, "I'm sorry, ma'am, but there's an age limit on beginning to live more fully."

So stop worrying about the "right" age for experiences. The worst that can happen is you'll have stories to tell—the kind that don't start with a nostalgic look back to when you were twenty-five.

The truth is: The only person who's been stopping you from leaping into new adventures is . . . well, you. You are your own built-in referee. And it's time to fire that gal/guy. Because if life is a game, you don't want to spend your later years as a benchwarmer.

In fact, I'm coming around to the idea that the back half of life is when the real fun kicks in. For me, aging is like leveling up in the game of life, unlocking new adventures and power-ups . . . also known as wisdom! It's like being handed a "Get Out of Overthinking Free" card—because at this point in my life I realize . . . ain't nobody got time for that!

Getting older has many definite perks.
- You know yourself more—*and care less about what people think*.
- You have the freedom to explore life with a deeper emotional and mental perspective—*that you didn't have when you were younger*.

The second half?

I believe it's about gathering all those rules you dutifully obeyed, then examining each with your mature eye, tilting your head, and saying, "Really?!" Then, one by one, you start breaking any rules you now recognize as absurd.

Why?

Because you can. And because, at this point, what do you really have to lose?

For my part, at this point in my life, I'm fully on board with no longer pretending to enjoy things I hate—like silent meditation retreats or kale chips. I believe that you can teach an old dog new tricks—because I'm learning lots of new tricks. Yes, I'm a dog in this scenario. Woof.

So go ahead and start a rock band in your sixties. Look for new love in your seventies. Or enroll in that pottery class, learn tap dancing—or even lap dancing! Because if you don't start daring to pursue your passions, you'll start feeling like you're trapped in a rerun of a show where the plot doesn't thicken, it just spreads out, thinner and less satisfying, into a watery soup of days.

Oh—and don't waste time beating yourself up about all the many people you wish you would have been—dancer you, baker you, mom you—a veritable chorus line of yous!

Know this now: To live is to pare down, to pick a lane.

Sometimes you choose. Sometimes the choice is a hurricane that picks you up and drops you somewhere you never planned. And there you are—landing with a thud—not even sure where your shoes went.

Make peace with your past.

Especially those parts where you didn't get to choose—because your choices were closed off by big, immovable things like time, money, or the laws of biology or physics.

You must soldier on—and ask yourself those questions that are sitting quietly in the back of your mind, too shy to raise their hands:

- What's tugging at my sleeve now?
- What am I pretending not to see and not to feel—that I truly, desperately want?
- What needs to be faced, embraced, or chased down by me?

Whatever the answer is, do it. Now. Because if you're not careful . . . before you know it . . . you will wake up one morning and realize you're not twenty-five anymore. In fact, you haven't been twenty-five for . . . well, let's not do the math.

Recognize that there are still many unexplored days ahead of you!

It's never too late to rejigger, to reframe, to reinvent. It's never too late to mess up, to start over, to laugh at yourself and say, "What the heck am I doing learning to tango at age seventy-one?" Then do it anyway.

After all, the only thing worse than starting something new and feeling foolish . . . is wishing that you did. Then feeling foolish because you didn't.

Because the truth is: It's going to break your heart later if you don't dare to try.

Remember: There is no expiration date on new beginnings.

It's time to toss out that rule book on when to stop starting. Get up off the couch and get started now. Yes, even if it means making those *"oooof"* sounds as you stand up. So what if your body creaks and groans a bit on the ascent? That's just the sound of your life machinery working—a sign you're still alive and moving. You're like a classic car. Maybe not as shiny as the newer models, but with an engine that still roars defiantly when you hit the gas.

You won't be alone in your daring late-bloomer adventures.

History's loaded up with folks who didn't get the memo that they were supposed to quietly decay after hitting fifty. There are many inspiring stories of people who said, "I'm not done yet!"

Some late-in-life beginners include:

- Colonel Sanders didn't strike it rich with his chicken empire until his sixties.
- Julia Child was fifty when she put out her first cookbook.
- Toni Morrison snagged a Nobel Prize in Literature at sixty-two.
- Grandma Moses didn't even start painting until she was in her seventies.
- Climbing Everest at seventy-three? Tamae Watanabe did that.
- Let's not forget about Morgan Freeman. This man didn't land his first major movie role until he was fifty-two.
- Plus John Glenn was seventy-seven when he ventured back into space.

You're never too old to pick up a brush, a pen, a microphone, a chicken wing . . . or whatever.

It's not just these famous giants either. I've seen people around me rewrite their stories later in life. Marla popped out a baby at fifty. Jane ditched her soul-crushing corporate job at forty-seven to chase her dream in sustainable fashion. John went back to school at fifty-one to become a therapist. Susie reignited her passion for photography in her fifties.

Plus there's my incredible mom.

After my dad passed away, she met her now long-term boyfriend Irv when she was in her seventies—then starred in a play at ninety-two.

Each of these stories are proof that blooming can happen at any age, that perhaps the richness of the soil improves—not in spite of the years—but because of them.

But you don't have to go humongous with your rejiggering.

After all, many of us don't have the luxury of starting over completely—of shedding our lives like last year's snakeskin. There are kids, half-raised, staring bewildered at algebra homework. There are jobs, two years shy of a pension.

As a result, many of us feel like we're handcuffed to mundane moments—because we're scheduled down to the minute. It's not like you can just drop everything and become a street artist in Paris, because who's going to drive mom to the chiropodist?

Who says starting small isn't starting at all?

Even with your commitments, you can still shape-shift your life a little! I'm not talking about completely abandoning ship—but about learning to dance on the deck!

Here's a wild thought:
- What if you became the world's okayest harmonica player?
- Or you started writing poetry that you only read to your dog?
- Perhaps you could try stand-up comedy at the local café on a Wednesday night.
- Or turn your garage into a painter's studio.

Rejiggering your life isn't merely about the grand leap.
- It's about the small steps taken—while the coffee brews or the laundry tumbles dry.
- It's grabbing a sketch pad or a set of watercolors and just making something.
- It's about finding those tiny moments of rebellion against the mundane—that don't require a grand departure from your current life.

This way, you can start to craft a life that feels more genuinely yours, even if the outward appearance hasn't changed much at all.

Rejiggering your life doesn't require a total overhaul—just a little tuning up, adjusting, recalibrating.

You're not trying to become someone else completely. You're just trying to be more you, more engaged, more interested, more interesting.

Think about those obituaries you've read—some of which sound like epic novels—lives brimming with raising babies, chairing committees, volunteering, singing in glee clubs, rescuing cats, growing vegetable gardens, traveling. Guess what? These were people who had other commitments too. They just found a way to fulfill their commitments—while fulfilling themselves as well.

Sure, joining the local choir won't turn you into Adele, but it might just be a blast singing your heart out. And maybe, just maybe, you'll inspire someone else to shake things up. You'll be setting off those ripples of inspiration, showing others it's possible to rejigger their lives too.

Plus . . . isn't rejiggering sorta the point of life?

You want to create a life so rich with quirky, personalized details—that when your eulogy is finally read aloud, it sounds less like a generic checklist and more like the poetic lyrics of a life well lived.

This balancing act—between duty and desire—isn't easy. But it's doable, with a bit of flair and a lot of stealth.

Now I hear you asking, "But how do I start?"

First, you must understand that fear is the main villain in your story. Fear of failure, of judgment, of change.

You must slap those fears in the face—with the following far bigger fear:

The regret of getting to the end of your life—and feeling like you wished you'd lived with more courage and passion.

Sure, habits can be hard to break. But the only thing that should ever be set in stone is that inscription on your future gravestone. And you have the power to make sure that this inscription does NOT read, "Here lies the King/Queen of Excuses."

Life is short. But it's also wide. You need to spread your arms, take a deep breath, and plunge into it headfirst.

Do it now. Because here's the deal: We're all going to die.

I know, shocking news. If you're just finding out now, I apologize. Although I've been trying my best to catch you up to speed on this.

If you've known about death for a while now—but still haven't done much with this information—now's the time to act! *Because the Grim Reaper is unbribable!*

The truth is: When you finally face the fact that your life has a hard stop, you'll wonder why you ever kept those pristine, unused sketchbooks on the shelf, when they could have been messy, inked with attempts at capturing the curve of a sleeping cat.

In the end it boils down to this:

If something is genuinely important to you, you'll find a way.

If not, you'll find an excuse.

It's time to start amping up your courage and dialing down your excuses!

TEN TOOLS TO REJIGGER YOUR LIFE

It's never too late to decide that things can be different, that they can be better. Here are some tools to help.

1. Think It—Then Shrink It

What do you want to add to your life? Painting? Carpentry? Learning to sing without making dogs howl? Break down your goal into small steps—so you turn this big, scary thing into smaller, chewable bits, like those cute mini cupcakes. Then "time box" your mini-cupcake-sized steps into your calendar—schedule them as if they were as critical as your yearly physical. Because in a way, they are.

2. Do a Daily Dare

Eleanor Roosevelt (supposedly) once said, "Do one thing every day that scares you." I love this idea. It's terrific for building up your courage muscles. Each day think of something brave to do. Try a new workout. Say hi to your neighbors. Go on a field trip to some new place that is sixty minutes away from your home. Build up your bravery muscles—one awkward, shaky courage lift at a time.

3. Create a Notebook of Small Experiments

Every week, jot down your progress on your rejiggering experiments. Cooked a new recipe? Took a different route to work? Listened to a new genre of music? This notebook will encourage you to stop living a life of Groundhog Day reruns. Because no one wants to live the same Tuesday on loop, no matter how good the coffee was.

4. Write Funny Morning News Headlines

Every morning, write down one humorous headline you'd like to see in your personal news.

- Local Man Finally Learns Spanish
- Woman Beats Own Record for Days in a Row Painting on a Canvas
- Woman Declares Victory over Procrastination and Starts Writing Novel
- Widower, 78, Joins Dating Scene—Says, "Excited to Love and Be Loved Again"

5. Buddy Up Like a Bank Heist

Find your partner in crime—figuratively, please. Team up with someone who is as eager to shake things up as you are. Make a pact to call each other out on any (b)lame excuses—and push each other to take bold steps. Think of this person as your bank heist buddy, but instead of stealing money, you're stealing time to do the things you wanna do.

6. Skill Swap

Know a friend who's got skills you envy? Swap skills with them! Maybe they know how to do yoga—but you know how to write poetry. Think of it as a mutual mentorship, a buddy system for the soul.

7. The Last Year Imagined

When fear and excuses start whispering in your ear, just ask yourself, "If I only had one year left to live, would I regret not doing this?" It's like getting a reality check from your future self—who is kind of bossy, but also surprisingly persuasive.

8. Call Me "Elder," Not "Elderly"

I love that many cultures call older people "elders," a term that comes with major clout. In fact, in many indigenous societies, these elders are the go-to folks for just about everything.

- Need advice on how to navigate a life crisis? *Check with the elders.*
- Wanna hear a good, inspiring story? *Pull up a chair by the elders.*

In these cultures, aging isn't a slow march toward irrelevance. It's a progression toward honor. Elders are revered for their wisdom, stories, and all they have to offer. Plus, they often report better mental health compared to their peers in other cultures.

So let's rewrite the script on aging, so it's less *fading away* and more *stepping into the spotlight.*

9. Find Your Third Place

There's this interesting concept conceived by sociologist Ray Oldenburg called the "third place," which is all about finding a physical place, other than your home or office, where you can feel like you're part of something.

Imagine a cozy bookstore that hosts book readings for a community of fellow book lovers, people who breathe books just like you.

Think about a dog park, where not only does everyone know your dog's name, but they know your name too.

And it doesn't stop there. Perhaps your third place is a synagogue, a church, a mosque, a yoga studio, a gym, a pottery class. Basically, your third place is a space where you feel connected, seen, and fully yourself.

10. Rewrite Your Aspirational Eulogy to Include What You're Rejiggering!

Remember that aspirational eulogy you've been writing? Time to dust it off again and give it a tune-up. Why? Because you're doing new rejiggering things, and they deserve to be documented.

As you update your aspirational eulogy, think to yourself, "Yes! I'm taking control of my life story! It's mine to write." Let yourself feel pride too—like, "Holy smokes, I'm actually going to live a life like this!"

Remember, your aspirational eulogy isn't meant for a future crowd of mourners. It's meant for YOU—right here, right now. Think of it as a rough draft that's never done—until your life is done! And as long as you're here, your life is far from done!

YOU CAN GET BETTER AND BETTER, NOT JUST OLDER AND OLDER.

Age isn't a cage—unless you let it be. So, f*ck fear. F*ck excuses. F*ck limiting beliefs. F*ck being afraid to spell out the word FUCK in a book! *(Yeah, I went there!)*

In fact . . . your later years can actually become your best years ever. And that's not just me trying to cheer you up. It's backed by research!

The U Shape of Happiness

Researchers at the University of Texas discovered that happiness follows a U shape over the course of life—kind of like a skateboard park. High on both ends, low in the middle. Here's the breakdown.

- **Youth?** That's when you're launching off the ramp, soaring high, fueled by energy, endless possibilities and the sheer joy of thinking you're invincible.
- **Then middle age hits.** And it's like someone filled your pockets with rocks—and also added a mortgage, a job you're not sure you like, and a marriage that might be teetering between rom-com and psychological thriller. And then there's your kids, who you know must love you—but have a hard time showing it. This is when the U dips. Big time.
- **Finally we become older.** Now's when things go on the upswing. Just when your knees give out, your happiness ticks up. It's not that you don't have problems anymore. You just know that you can handle them. Or you know which ones to let go of. And so you find this weird little thing called inner peace.

This U-shaped curve of happiness reminds me of a quote from the philosopher Arthur Schopenhauer:

"Life may be compared to a piece of embroidery, of which, during the first half of his time, a man gets a sight of the right side, and during the second half, of the wrong. The wrong side is not so pretty as the right, but it is more instructive; it shows the way in which the threads have been worked together."

What Schopenhauer is saying fits perfectly with this U-curve.

When you're young, all you see is the polished front side of life. But as you age, you start to see the messy underside—the knots, tangles, and loose threads. At first it's jarring. But then you realize it's a kind of map. Those messy bits explain why the chaotic and beautiful parts interplayed the way they did.

Hopefully, in your later years, you'll start to see your life like that. Not perfect, but stitched together in a way that makes sense—eventually.

Time to start rejiggering.

Alright, so here we are, at the end of this chapter. You've got your goals, tools, and a kick-in-the-tush reminder that you are not fixed, but fluid. You can reimagine, reinvent, and reinvigorate your life at any point.

Now it's time to start moving.

Because you don't stop dancing because you get old. You get old because you stop dancing. And I don't know about you, but I plan on dancing—awkwardly and enthusiastically—for a long time to come.

22

MISTAKES WERE MADE:
A REALISTIC GUIDE TO FORGIVENESS

Recently I was out to dinner with my family. I excused myself to go to the restroom and found something very interesting scribbled on the bathroom wall:

Lynn + men who don't love her

Although I chuckled, I also felt Lynn's pain. Over a decade ago, I experienced bad patterns in love, which thankfully I've since broken.

I used to joke that if we all had a one-in-a-million chance of meeting the right guy, I only had about two or three guys left to go out with. I felt like I'd dated nearly every eligible (and *non-eligible*) man in New York City.

Sitting there, in the dim light of that restroom, I was tempted to write back a helpful note to Lynn, right below her scribble:

Lynn + men who are just stand-ins for unresolved issues from her past

Basically, I wanted to remind Lynn that she needed to own her lessons in her bad love pattern—in order to disown her bad love pattern.

Unfortunately, Lynn's bathroom graffiti seemed to suggest that she thought there was no logic to her pain—and that the universe had randomly handplucked her for torture.

Consider how she worded her love problem: Lynn + men who don't love her

Ironically, how Lynn viewed her problem . . . *was exactly her problem!*

There's a saying: "We repeat what we don't repair."

Lynn, it seemed, was on repeat for a non-repaired issue. Basically, Lynn was not breaking any new romance ground because she was digging that same familiar hole deeper . . . and deeper.

Admittedly, it's hard to let go of our pain from the past.

But you can at least make sure you don't make your painful story your dominant narrative, like Lynn did. And like so many people do.

How do you know you have a painful dominant narrative?

Well, you might find yourself telling a story that begins with, "My life is ruined because . . ."

For example . . .
- My life is ruined because I had a narcissistic parent.
- My life is ruined because I miscarried.
- My life is ruined because my dad died/left when I was young.

Or you might have a story on repeat mode with the words "always" or "never."
- I can never make money.
- I always meet women who lie and cheat.

Yes, yes, yes, these are all terrible tragedies. *Traumas, even.*

Yes, yes, yes, your feelings of pain and heartache about your past pain are valid. *Exceptionally valid, even.*

But when you make a painful story your dominant narrative instead of just a *part* of your narrative, you wind up keeping yourself stuck in a repetitive pain loop. And this can lead to further struggles.

Think of it like this:
- You wouldn't let someone who's feeling road rage drive your car, right?
- So why let old pains steer your life?

Instead, you must acknowledge your painful feelings. Learn and grow from them. But then gently—and firmly—guide them to the back seat, so you can take the wheel of your life.

You must start challenging the "I'm just a person who sucks at life" storyline. And find evidence that you don't entirely suck.

Know this now: When you stop telling your story as if it is a sad one . . . eventually it will stop being a sad one.

Coming up, I'm going to walk you through how to better spot your dominant narratives. Plus, I'll share a process to rewrite yours—using something called "life review therapy."

Life review therapy will help you to see:
- You are not the unfortunate series of events and traumas that you've faced.
- You're not your failed tests, the broken relationships, the lost opportunities.
- Maybe you played a role in some of your challenges. Maybe you didn't.
- Either way . . . you should not define your life by a painful dominant narrative.

Remember this: Time is a nonrenewable resource. You're only here temporarily. So you must stop filling your temporary life with permanent resentment and perpetual sorrow.

Think about it. If the world were to end tomorrow . . .
- Would you rather spend tonight being pissed off about your past?
- Or would you rather watch one last sunset with a glass of decent wine, enjoying the company of a loved one?

My mission: Make sure you choose the latter.

The upcoming process: You're going to review your life, note the patterns, spot the lessons, appreciate the good stuff—and do some forgiveness.

Oh—and if you're eye-rolling at the word "forgiveness"—please stop. I encourage you to give it a try. It's essential. And it's time.

To illustrate the importance of forgiveness, let me introduce you to Siddhartha Mukherjee, a Pulitzer Prize–winning author and oncologist who spends his days in cancer wards hearing people's final words at their final moments.

Mukherjee reports, "Every person that I've met in this moment of transition wanted to make four offerings."

These are:

- "I want to tell you that I love you."
- "I want to tell you that I forgive you."
- "Would you tell me that you love me?"
- "Would you give me your forgiveness?"

Yep, Mukherjee says that in those final moments, people are scrambling to make things right. They're seeking forgiveness—or asking for it—eager to feel love and peace in their hearts.

I believe we shouldn't wait till our deathbeds to free our hearts from anger, regret, shame, and guilt!

Instead, we should live our lives now with this "deathbed clarity" in mind.

So it's time to forgive them. All of your "thems." (Yes, even *that* one.) The more "thems" you can forgive . . . the better you'll feel. And yes, this also includes forgiving yourself!*

Forgiveness is an act of self-care and self-respect. It's like saying, "I don't need this subplot of anger and resentment in my story anymore. I'm going for a happier storyline."

Unfortunately, in order to heal the pain of your past, you must dig around in the muck of your life—to gain insights and reframe your story.

That's where life review therapy comes in.

This process is like hitting rewind on a movie to understand the plot better. It involves reflecting on your life and finding purpose and meaning in your pain, so you can achieve a sense of closure.

---

* Admittedly, the heart can be a bit of a hoarder, stockpiling grudges, harsh words, and past pain, as if each were a priceless artifact rather than a ticket stub to a show that's long since ended. Unfortunately, these keepsakes take up precious space where new joy could be doing cartwheels. And so we need to recognize that every past hurt is not meant to be a tenant with a lease, but merely a traveler just passing through.

Traditionally, life review therapy (LRT) involves sitting with a therapist who helps you to navigate your memories. But coming up, I'm offering you a DIY version—a self-guided tour through the landscape of your past—armed with curiosity, introspection, honesty, and a hefty dose of empathic self-love.

Remember, nobody expects you to turn into the Dalai Lama after your first go at this. LRT is a practice that unfolds over time. But stick with it, and eventually you'll stop telling your story as a sad one—and ultimately, it will not feel so sad at all.

So, how does this life review therapy thing work?

You start with something called "chronological mapping"—where you literally map out a timeline of your life on the biggest piece of paper you can find. And I'm not talking 8.5 by 11. No, I mean something huge, like a roll of butcher paper. Go big.

Lay the paper out horizontally. Next, I want you to start drawing a long line—stretching from one end of this absurdly large paper to the other. Then fill in key details on your life timeline by making a huge dot for each pivotal moment, those highs that made your heart soar and those lows that felt like emotional potholes. Next to each dot write simple phrases. "Started high school." "Lost my first job." "Had my heart ripped out and stomped on." You get the idea.

You can start adding notes at the left end of the page, at your earliest memory, then gradually move to the right, where today's version of you hangs out. Or don't be linear at all. Just jump around like you're on some kind of time-travel bender. There's no wrong way to do this. The goal is just to brainstorm the moments that made you go, *"Well, that changed things."* Firsts, lasts, triumphs, disasters—the big "aha!" moments.

Once you've got your timeline dotted and labeled, keep going. Add notes about what happened, who was there, and how it felt. Did it change you? Did it break you? Did it build you?

Draw doodles or symbols to mark various occasions. A star for the highs. Maybe a teardrop for the lows. A heart for love. A dollar sign for money. Or use colored markers to note patterns. Then make a key on the side of the paper, like you're creating a map to your own emotional treasure chest.

Digging through your past like this might feel like an emotional Indiana Jones adventure. Sometimes you'll unearth happy treasures you forgot about. Other times, you'll stumble into emotional quicksand traps.

Whenever you find yourself recalling a painful memory, I want you to pause, stand back, and look at the huge timeline in front of you. Tell yourself, "Okay, that particular life chapter sucked, but here's what it taught me." Then scribble down the life lessons each event offered up (or smacked you with). Describe the various feelings and core values that you embraced most during these times. Did you become more patient? Braver? A little more wonderfully weird? Note how everything sculpted the person you've become.

Important: Don't deny or alter the reality of your life. Just to try to shift your perspective a bit, like tilting your head to see the picture hidden in one of those Magic Eye posters. Soon you'll view your life with a deeper understanding.

This exercise doesn't mean you'll suddenly see every terrible thing as a hidden blessing. Life's not that simple. You can't always find a silver lining in every cloud. But you can recognize that the sun is as much a part of your life's landscape as those clouds.

Your goal: Stop allowing a painful dominant narrative from your past to hijack your present.

Here are some things to ponder as you do your chronological mapping.
- What are the recurring themes or patterns in my life—and why might I have developed them?
- What lessons have I learned from mistakes, obstacles, pain, challenges, and traumas?
- In what ways have I grown or changed over the years?
- What unresolved issues still linger that I need to address?
- Are there apologies I need to make or accept from others?
- What would I have done differently—knowing what I know now?

Other methods to try:
Rename the painful times in your life as "the gift" or "the assignment." Write down those words on your chronological map. Then dig through your challenges and try to find the hidden "gift of insight" or the buried "gift of inner

strength." Or be on the lookout for that time-delayed "assignment of wisdom" or that camouflaged "assignment of self-respect."

You can also rename your challenging events as "the bridge" or "the zigzag." Then look at your chronological map, and explore how your tough times wound up leading you to better places that you might not have otherwise reached. Did a heartbreak zigzag you into a better relationship? Did getting fired build a bridge to a more-right-for-you job?

Remind yourself: The pain you're replaying in your mind isn't necessarily the truth. It's just one version of your story, a version you've decided to cling to like a bad narrator. The truth is, there are a million ways to interpret your life—some are hopeful, some are downright cruel. Stop choosing the cruelest interpretations.

LRT will help you view life with "pain-a-ramic vision."

After working through this process, you'll see the whole picture of your life—with a full 360-degree lens. You'll stop viewing yourself as a perpetual victim of bad luck or poor decisions. Instead, you'll become the proactive protagonist of your story—someone who learned, healed, grew, and, most importantly, kept going.

But after you're done—you're still not done!

Next it's time to write something called a "personal acceptance narrative."

Grab your journal. I want you write a more positive dominant narrative about yourself to replace the negative one.

Describe yourself as the hero of your story—someone who went through ups and downs, made mistakes, learned from them, faced challenges, overcame them, fell sometimes . . . but always got up stronger. When you're done, sign it. Seriously. Sign it like you're making a contract with yourself, because you are. This is your new reality: to view pain as something to learn from, not wallow in.

Here's the deal going forward:

Every time you find your mind wandering back to your old, negative dominant narrative, I want you to do a stop and swap.

- Stop saying, "My life is ruined because . . ."
- Swap in: "I learned something important about myself from that event—and it led me to a better place, which I'm committed to enjoying now."

Example from My Own Life

Back when I was in my thirties, I met this guy who I thought was intoxicating. Turns out I was wrong by a few syllables. He was just plain ol' toxic. Let's call him Tox to protect his identity.

Even though I knew Tox was a lethal combo of trouble and troubled, when we broke up I felt as if my Plan A life had been pulled out from under me. I wondered how it would ever be possible to find a happy Plan B storyline.

My negative dominant narrative:

This breakup is the beginning of my descent into "unhappily ever after."

Pretty bleak, right?

But after doing this LRT process, I was able to reframe my heartbreak into a hero's journey story. I recognized that:

Yeah, this past relationship was a doozy, but it taught me to trust my gut.

Thanks to Tox, I made a non-negotiable promise to myself: I will never again shrink myself, warp myself, or play emotional Twister just to make a bad relationship "work."

These weren't simply happy little lies. They were true pieces of wisdom— that I managed to scrape out of the wreckage—and use to rebuild myself into someone far better at giving and receiving love.

In fact, thanks to that painful breakup, I didn't just become a better partner, I became a better everything: friend, mom, daughter, colleague, human being. So yeah, Tox sucked. But oddly enough, I owe him a thank-you card for making me better.

LRT works like a narrative reframing machine.

You feed in the sob stories, and what pops out isn't a shiny fairy tale, but something real. It's still got the rough edges. But now it's a personal acceptance narrative of growth, not defeat. A human adventure, not a tragedy. A journey of self-discovery.

In my case, I stopped telling myself, "This breakup's a redirection toward unhappily ever after."

Instead, I swapped in this personal acceptance narrative: "I didn't lose love. I lost a bad habit. I let go of something that wasn't right for me, and in doing so, made room for far more fulfilling love."

After I crafted this new positive dominant narrative, I wove it into my aspirational eulogy, like this ...

"Karen is someone who didn't just stumble through life; she mindfully learned from each fall. She used her missteps as stepping stones, and thereby she taught us all a thing or two about resilience and personal growth."

Struggling to Make Your Negative Dominant Narrative Less Domineering?

Here's another empowering tool— taken from my own tool belt.

After my breakup with Tox, I told myself the following powerful sentence—which helped me to stop viewing the breakup as a gigantic life sentence:

The part is not greater than the whole.

This is a mathematical principle based in fact—which also applies to life. Think about it. A breakup is just a slice of one's life. It is not one's whole life pie.

Nothing is everything.

- A breakup is not everything.
- A challenging event of any kind is not everything.
- A tough time is merely something going on INSIDE one's life!
- A hard time is NOT one's WHOLE life.
- It's just a slice—not the whole!
- And there are still many other yummy parts of life to enjoy.

I recognize that these exercises are not easy. But letting go of your negative dominant narrative will be one of the most fulfilling things you can do for yourself.

Do it now. Because let's face it—the real tragedy isn't that life is short. It's that we spend too much time repeating our regrets—instead of performing our recovery.

NEXT UP ... LET'S TALK ABOUT EMOTIONAL RECONCILIATION

After you're done with this LRT process, you might discover that you're open to forgiving someone. You might even see that you played a role in a past drama—and you want to ask for forgiveness. Or you might simply want to talk about everything with someone who hurt you now that there's been a buffer of time.

If you do feel tempted to reach out to someone, please remember: Not every relationship is fixable.

Some bridges are too burned to cross again. And that's okay.

Sometimes all that matters is that you tried. That's the real win—knowing you made an effort. Because you *don't* want to wind up on your deathbed, haunted by the question, *"What if I'd just reached out?"*

If the idea of a phone call (or text) is too much, try writing a letter.

Pour everything out onto the page: how you feel, what you wish had been different. This is a terrific way to organize your thoughts, to see them in black and white, which might make them easier to understand or accept.

Once it's all down, you can decide whether to send the letter, tuck it away, or let it burn in an ashtray. Sometimes the mere act of writing can untether you from the past, offering the closure that a conversation might not.

Struggling to Forgive?

Even after LRT, you might feel like forgiveness is forever off the table. Maybe what they did was truly awful, and you're thinking, *No way am I letting them off the hook for the spiritual debt they owe me.*

This is often why people are tempted to pursue revenge—as a method to even out the score. But doing an act of revenge only dirties up your side of the street—which dirties up your sense of self.

Letting go of anger is the cleanest way to move forward.

Forgiveness is making the decision not to roll around in your offender's mud. It's choosing to release your offender from their spiritual debt so you can invest your thoughts and energy more wisely. And here's the best part: By letting go, you avoid racking up your own emotional debt—those late fees of anger and resentment that often feel worse than the original offense.

Here's how to cancel all debts:

First, write down everything that person did that's eating you up.

Then, one by one, cross those things out. Write "canceled" or "paid in full" next to each one.

Remember:

As long as you're hating someone, you're keeping them important. Forgive them and you make them obsolete.

Still Struggling to Forgive?

Here's a tool I discovered by accident. It's simple and truly works.

As I mentioned earlier, I like to call my son "Little Handsome." But I have another nickname for him too:

My reset button.

I've never said this out loud—not to his face, not to anyone. But for many years now, I've had the feeling of my son being my reset button.

What does this mean?

It means I can forgive any forehead-slapping mistake I made before my son was born. Because every single thing—every heartbreak, every dumb-ass business move, every idiotic real estate deal—had to happen exactly as it did . . . in order for my son to exist.

And I absolutely feel a palooza of gratitude for giving birth to my son.

And so his birth reset everything, erasing all regrets from before August 2010 (when he arrived into this world).

If you're struggling to forgive yourself—or someone else—pause and ask:

- What are my reset buttons?
- Do I acknowledge my reset buttons with the appropriate gratitude and revelry?

Next time you catch yourself mumbling a negative dominant narrative, simply reach for your reset button. It will help to erase any nagging doubts about why things had to happen as they did.

Life's too short for regrets—and far too short for lifelong resentment.

In the grand scheme of things, our time is limited. So don't let your grievances live longer than you do.

23

HOW TO FALL BACK IN LOVE WITH LIFE

Here's a brain teaser for you:

If you could live your life for the next ten years in complete and total happiness—no emotional pain whatsoever—but in the end, not remember any of it, would you do it?

Let me clarify: no struggles, no pain, just pure bliss for a decade. Then *poof*—it's like it never happened.

Tempting? Not to me. In fact, I'd like to make a case for the importance of emotional pain. Plus, I'd like to make a second case for taking lots of time to sit with your pain.

No, I'm not a masochist.

I'm someone who believes that the point of life is to learn as much as you can from your pain—so you can grow as much as you can.

Basically, I believe that life isn't supposed to be just a "den of pleasure." It's also a "laboratory of growth." That's where you test things out, mess things up, and figure out how to become the best version of yourself.

Unfortunately, too many people make it their goal to spend their entire life hanging out in the den of pleasure. They're resistant to wandering into the lab of growth to do the necessary work.

But it's not realistic to live in a perpetual state of joy. Life isn't constant sunshine. It's a mix of sunshine and storms. Ebbs and flows.

Unfortunately, life can sometimes feel like ebb, ebb, ebb; brief flash of flow; more ebb, ebb, ebb. But every ebb offers you something. A new perspective. A new skill. A new way of seeing the world.

This isn't just me waxing poetic about the benefits of tough times. There's solid science backing this up—in an area psychologists call "emodiversity."

Emodiversity is short for "emotional diversity." It's a theory that explains how we humans need the full spectrum of emotions in order to be happy—everything from the good to the crappy. Turns out, letting yourself feel pissed off or downright depressed can actually *help* you in the long run.

According to research on emotional diversity:

Adults who experience a greater diversity of both positive and negative emotions report fewer symptoms of depression and fewer days spent in a hospital.

You read that correctly! Ironically, spending time processing uncomfortable emotions can lead to less overall depression and better health. I know, it sounds backward—like eating cake to lose weight.

So, why does emotional diversity work?

Well, studies reveal it helps you to bulk up your emotional resilience, much like muscles built through resistance training. Every time you actively engage with negative feelings, you're strengthening your ability to find meaning in life's pain and buffing up your personal growth.

The payoff? Better mental health and more authentic happiness—with a depth to your joy that you can't get from lounging around in the den of pleasure.

As I've mentioned earlier, Aristotle, my go-to philosopher for life advice, calls this deeper feeling of happiness "eudaimonia." Roughly translated, it means "flourishing as your highest self."

Quickie refresher from chapter 8:

- **Hedonia** is about pursuing ego-directed and body-directed immediate gratification—the kind you get lounging in the den of pleasure.
- **Eudaimonia** is about engaging in soul-directed and growth-directed habits that lead to deeper, more meaningful joy —the kind you discover in the lab of growth.

Aristotle preached about the perks of eudaimonia. He argued that true happiness doesn't come from superficial immediate pleasures (sorry, hedonia fans). Instead, it's earned by putting in some effort—and stepping into your true greatness, one challenging step at a time.

Aristotle's take: True happiness isn't a shiny trophy you get after you solve life's maze. It's the strength you build while you're stumbling through it.

And so Aristotle was ahead of his time because he was a fan of the counterintuitive benefits of emodiversity—many centuries before that term was ever coined.

Psychologists have this metaphor they love to trot out to describe the benefits of emodiversity: They compare emodiversity to biodiversity in nature.

Think of a forest. For a tree to grow at its best, it needs other trees, moss, mushrooms, birds, bugs, bacteria, and, yeah, even some weird creepy-crawlies. It's messy. A little gross. But everything adds something vital. The other trees give shade, the bugs break down waste, the fungi help things flourish. Everything's working together, balancing out the ecosystem.

Psychologists say we humans need emotional diversity for the same reason nature needs biodiversity. For us to truly thrive, we need the whole wild jungle of emotions—anger, sadness, frustration. Because it's not just the sunny days that help us grow. It's weathering the storms.

This brings me to a core belief of mine (inspired by Aristotle):
The point of life is NOT to live pain free.
The point of life is to grow into your best self.

When you choose to be mentally strong during tough times you can morph life's garbage into gold—and wind up evolving into your best self.

In many ways this topic of emotional diversity reminds me of something Viktor Frankl wrote about in his book *Man's Search for Meaning*.

Frankl said, "There is meaning and value in suffering. Challenges help you to become something greater than you might have been."

Or as I like to say:
Often it's your deepest pain that inspires you to grow into your highest self.

And so it's okay if you are NOT happy every single day of your life. It's okay if you only seize every third day. As long as you spend some time in that lab of growth, digging around in the crappy stuff of life, looking for those sparkling gems of insight, gratitude, purpose, and growth.

William James, the philosopher, wrote about this too, in his own unique way. He said there are two kinds of people: once-born and twice-born. And he made a strong case for becoming twice-born.

Once-born people are folks who never want to wander too far from the safety of their known world. When a crisis arrives, pushing once-born people into darkness, they simply choose to sit in the dark rather than flip on that self-illumination switch. As a result, they miss out on finding those hidden gems of insight and bursts of growth.

Twice-born people, in contrast, love to use a shake-up in their outer world as an opportunity to wake up their inner world. They seek a more profound view on life—and their purpose and potential in it. They view crisis pain as a fiery trial that burns away the old and paves the way for a new, better version of themselves.

I've always loved James's definition of twice-born people and have tried my best to join their ranks. Although by now, I think I've graduated to the twentieth-born tribe.

Let me tell you . . . *I've had my share of wild challenges!* One of the greatest (and most hilariously wrong) compliments I ever got was when someone said they thought my life had been easy. I chuckled— because my life has been miles from easy.

I've been through so many adversities that I started calling them "my bucket list from hell."

This list is not to be confused with a normal bucket list. I didn't do fun things like "trek the Inca Trail." No, no! It was as if by accident I got my hands on a bizarro-world bucket list. Then, diligent me, I managed to meticulously check off a wide range of heartbreaking, soul-crushing, serotonin-depleting incidents!

I've written about these painful times in *The Bounce Back Book*—and how I don't regret a thing. Because in the end there was time-delayed wisdom and joy to be found in each of those painful experiences!

Thanks to my bucket list from hell, I wound up blooming into who I am today. And I truly feel wiser, stronger—and even more loving—because of all I endured. Plus now I appreciate all that I have—and all *whom* I have—with so much extra gusto.

In the end I took all those broken pieces of my life and did my best to build something beautiful out of it all.

I confess it was a challenging journey to get from that hell to here.

There were many "you-gotta-be-freaking-kidding-me" tough moments—when I could not find the will to laugh nor the strength to get up from the sofa. I'd simply lie there in the fetal position, feeling as if someone hit the off switch for my brain, my heart, my personality.

Maybe you've felt like that too? Like you're not just swimming against the tide but caught in a rip current that is dragging you into a swirling vortex of despair.

That's called "survival mode."

When you're in survival mode, it's like you're at war with the world. Every day is a battle. You feel like you're trapped in a 24/7 marathon of *The Walking Dead*—except you're both the terrified humans and the mindless zombies. You feel exhausted, beaten down, like there's no end in sight.

If you're stuck in survival mode right now, I'm here to help. This chapter is meant to gently guide you into the lab of growth so you can find your way back to faith and fulfillment.

Know this now:

The greatest stories ever told have been about people—from Odysseus to Batman—who hit rock bottom only to bounce back higher than ever before.

Every great story has its tensions, its disasters, its resolutions. So think of yourself as being in the throes of discovering that important plot twist, inching yourself closer to that resolution where you'll come out on top.

Here's a story to support this optimistic lens:

J.K. Rowling, author of the billion-dollar-making Harry Potter series, didn't get to where she is by having an easy ride. She went through the wringer, as a broke single mom, experiencing failure after failure. Her missteps? They were what led her to write one of the most influential book series of our time.

In fact, when Rowling gave her commencement speech at Harvard, she didn't gush about the success of Harry Potter. She talked about the benefits of failure. Why? Because her failures stripped away the inessential, allowing her to focus on her true passion of writing.

This brings me to some important points.

- Rowling isn't just famous for her fictional story about a boy wizard. She's just as famous for her *real-life* story of overcoming adversity.
- Her survival story is so powerful, it's become her inspiring legacy story—which helps others to survive their tough times too.

How does this apply to you?

You too can take the survival mode story you're presently struggling with—and mindfully rewrite it as a legacy story to inspire others.

How do you morph your pain into this purpose?

My answer is (*no shocker here*): Think about death.

Are you in the midst of survival mode now? Do this deathbed meditation.

1. Visualize your future self, many years down the line, on your deathbed.
2. Ask yourself: Do I want my future self to be proud of how I handled my adversities—because I faced my challenges head-on and used them as stepping stones to a better life? Or . . .
3. Do I want my future self to remember how I folded under pressure, gave in to survival mode, and let the stress chew me up?

Use your crisis pain as crisis fuel.

Envision your future self cheering you on, urging you: "Make those right choices that'll make me proud!"

Important reminder:

On your deathbed, you're not only going to remember the beautiful sunsets and the giddy first kisses.

You're also going to remember those battles you fought, the mountains you climbed, and the dragons you slayed—or at least the dragons you told to buzz off.

My wish for you: When you're counting your final breaths, you'll be grinning with gratitude, knowing you turned your survival mode time into a springboard for growth and, ultimately, a life well lived.

TOOLS FOR SURVIVAL

Admittedly, right now you might be thinking, "Yeah, right, lady, easier said than done!"

So I've got some tools to help you to get it done.

Survival Mode Tool #1: Seeing the Ugly

When you find yourself spiraling into survival mode, don't deny it. Instead, breathe and acknowledge what's happening: "Ah, there you are, survival mode. I see you."

Sure, you're not thrilled, but you must acknowledge the pain—and not immediately try to numb it. This is your first step toward regaining control. You must stare your pain right in its ugly mug, give it a mental nod, and say, "I see you, and I'm not afraid of you, because I've got the tools to handle you. I am stronger than this challenge, and this challenge will make me even stronger."

And for the love of all that is good in this world . . . please stop shaming yourself for the pain you are wrestling with. Self-flagellation is no hobby for the sane. Pain upon pain is a math that just doesn't add up.

You deserve your own love and compassion. So love yourself fiercely. Sit with your discomfort. Hold it gently, like an injured bird, knowing it's meant to fly away . . . *when it's ready.*

Lovingly remind yourself:

It's not the bad days that define you—but how you choose to rise from them.

Survival Mode Tool #2: Cognitive Flexibility

Life isn't black and white (aka either disastrous or fantastic). There's a whole lot of gray—even if sometimes you gotta squint to see it. And that's where cognitive flexibility comes in! It grants you the mental chops to find that sliver of grayish light at the end of a super long, dark tunnel. Cognitive flexibility is about reframing your thoughts—until you start believing that no matter how messed up things may look, it's all gonna work out just fine.

Yes, even when every piece of evidence is screaming, "You're screwed!"

Research studies report: Embracing cognitive flexibility leads to greater tolerance of uncertainty and to improved mental health.

How do you become cognitively flexible?

You must swap out "Why me?" and "Why didn't I?" for more healing questions:

- What is this survival mode trying to teach me?
- What life patterns is this crisis highlighting that I need to change?
- How can I turn this turmoil into a chance to improve my life?
- What parts of my life do I need to let go of?

Next, reframe your vocabulary more positively. Stop thinking of survival mode as your nemesis. Start viewing it as your system reboot for your life.

Or tell yourself:

Similar to leg day at the gym, this time might be painful—but it's actually building your strength.

Or fill in this blank:

Lucky unlucky me, thanks to this challenging time, I'm being led toward some great things, like _____.

Then keep your eyes open for positive redirections!

But . . . don't just stop there!

Dig deep for some philosophical or spiritual positive backup during these rough patches.

Some folks lean on their religious faith. Others draw strength from philosophies like Stoicism or Buddhism. Find whatever works for you. God, destiny, universal energy, positive vibes, the power of love, good-karma-points-coming-your-way, angels, spirituality, everything-happens-for-a-reason-ism.

It doesn't matter the name you call it. All that matters is that you call upon it. Be grateful for its power to offer you buoyancy and faith.

Next up . . . If you're dealing with repeated patterns of pain, you need to take time to understand why. Here's a tool to help you to get to the bottom of things.

Survival Mode Tool #3:
Unshackling Yourself from Masochistic Equilibrium

"Masochistic equilibrium" is a fancy term for a pretty simple, yet screwed-up, psychological phenomenon where people sabotage their own happiness because, in a weird way, their discomfort feels like comfort.

Here's the lowdown:

From the time you were a kid, you picked up cues on what love and happiness look and feel like—based on your family dynamics. Let's say love in your household came bundled with yelling and insults. Fast forward to adulthood, and you somehow land in a calm, compliment-filled relationship. What happens? Your anxiety skyrockets—because calm and kind don't match the blueprint.

If you grew up used to chaos, then too much peace will feel alien. You'll then itch to sabotage things—in order to bring things back *down, down, down* to your familiar unhappiness zone—your normal-for-you emotional state— your masochistic equilibrium.

Or you might simply choose high-drama scenarios from the get-go—because your internal settings are stuck on disaster mode, and anything less just doesn't compute.

Freud named this urge for duplicating our past "repetition compulsion."

He explained how we humans have two methods to keep our past alive:

- Our thoughts—overdoing our daily thinking about our past
- Our actions—choosing current situations that are doppelgangers to our past

It's as if you have a portable childhood you take with you into adulthood. And you then try to cast new people in old family roles. So if you had a mom who was very *Mommie Dearest*—and shrieked at you all the time—you will attempt to create "Shriek Two: The Saga Continues."

Basically, a lot of the struggles in your life might be a sequel you unwittingly greenlit.

What's the fix?

You must accept that a lot of the painful events in your life might have been created by you—because of your negative childhood brainwashing. Or rather *braindirtying*. Because your lens to the world became *dirtied* with negative beliefs.

However, since you're older now, it's time to be wiser.

You must mindfully wipe your braindirtied lens clean—so you can more clearly see new paths to the life you desire—and deserve.

This is where my recommended "I am and so I do" statements come in handy.

You must ask yourself, "Who do I need to become to break free from this pattern of pain?"

Take time to actually think about it. Journal about it. Or better yet, go for a walk. And I don't mean a stroll to the fridge to check if there's still cake. I mean a real walk. Outside. Put one foot in front of the other. Walking can be a form of meditation, a way to get the blood flowing to your brain . . . so you come up with needed insights.

Speaking of "insights," here's an interesting tidbit:

Aristotle believed the highest form of knowledge is insight. He even ranked it above any knowledge you could get from a book or schooling.

Why? Because Aristotle recognized that "insight" is the only knowledge that leads to the education of your soul. And he believed that growing into your best self is the secret to true happiness.

Why chase insights when you're in a crisis?

Because survival mode isn't just a panic room. It's a treasure cave.

When you're fighting through survival mode, you're stripped down to the basics. And that's when you're most likely gonna learn the real, raw truths about yourself and your life. So be sure to mine these gritty times for those golden insights.

Next up, grab life by your core values.

Your core values are your life rafts during life's storms. They can keep you afloat.

Admittedly, living out your core values while in survival mode is hard. Heck, it's tough enough when things are going well. But it's the most rewarding thing you can do. Because when you live in alignment with your core values, you're aiming yourself at your highest potential life.

Here are two core values to particularly focus on during hard times.

Survival Mode Tool #4: Embracing Gratitude and Fun

Here's why it's hard to find happiness during survival mode:

Most people tend to think of happiness as a huge, slippery fish—one that you need to reel in by acquiring all kinds of bait, like money, abs, a house with a mudroom.

But, in reality, happiness is more like minnows, tiny, darting bits of joy, swimming around your ankles, unnoticed, because you're too busy scanning the horizon for something bigger.

If you want to find happiness during tough times, you gotta take your eyes off that distant horizon and look closer. Find the small things in front of you right now.

Sure, life is loaded up with bills, breakups, bad news . . . and a bunch of other bad *b* words. But it's also stuffed with things to be grateful for.

Train yourself to be a gratitude collector of joyful moments.
- The way your dog greets you like you're a Beatles reunion tour
- The smell of rain on warm pavement
- That first sip of coffee that tastes like a high-five to your soul

These aren't just consolation prizes while you wait for the big win. They're real-deal happiness—hidden in plain sight.

When life feels hard, cut down on the overthinking—and start over-thanking!

You've got 1,440 minutes in a day. Use at least five of them to focus on gratitude.

Here's the thing about life: Most days aren't fireworks or standing ovations. Most days are ordinary. If you're always waiting for something big in order to feel happy, you're not living—you're just loitering. And life is too weird and wonderful to just spend it in limbo waiting.

You must learn to find joy on ordinary days—not just on the days when you're sipping margaritas on a beach. Because if you're simply surviving until your next vacation . . . trust me, those margaritas won't taste as sweet if that's your only source of joy.

Next on the Agenda . . . Let's Dive into That Core Value: Fun!
When life feels like a conveyor belt of gloom, it's crucial to pepper your days with fun. Fun isn't just kids' stuff. It's survival gear for adults. In fact, sometimes fun and laughter are the very things that keep you sane when life keeps throwing those punches. They help you to counterpunch right back!

I'm such an advocate for fun that I gave a TEDx Talk titled "Fun Is a High-Performance Fuel." In it, I shared research all about the many perks of fun—how it eases tension, boosts your immune system, and helps you to problem solve better.

In many ways, fun is like meditation on steroids!
So when the world feels like it's closing in, ask yourself:
What fun thing can I do right here, right now—to feel better in this moment?
Then create an "I am and so I do" statement that pairs a core value with a fun habit:

- I am spontaneous, and so I take road trips without a plan.
- I am curious, and so I explore my city like a tourist.
- I am compassionate, and so I spend a day volunteering at an animal shelter—because puppies and kittens—duh.

When you start looking for fun, you'll find it hiding in places you didn't expect. And once fun sneaks back into your life, something else will too: humor.

Humor is a terrific enlightening agent, encouraging you to go from haha to aha.

Humor gives you this necessary distance. It's like stepping back from a painting—so you can see the whole picture, not just the ugly parts. Humor reminds you there's more to your life's canvas than the smudges you've been staring at.

So when the going gets tough, ask yourself:
Where's the humorous angle here?
I personally love to reframe my bad times with humor. So much so, I developed this quirky habit of having funny conversations with the Universe—as if it's a character in my life. I'll say things like, *"Really, Universe? Was it something I said?"*

One time I decided to write a long funny "Complaint Letter to the Universe"— as a way to let off steam.

Here's what I wrote:

Dear Universe,

I don't want to go through any more "what doesn't kill you will make you stronger" kinda stuff. So I'm writing to request a slight alteration to the program you've got running on my life ... perhaps a bug fix or software update.

While I am all for personal growth, I feel your "character building" department is getting a bit carried away with my storyline.

If I may offer a bit of friendly advice, Universe ... Let's talk pacing. Ever heard of it? It's this cool literary technique where not everything happens at once. Maybe we could pace out the life lessons like a TV show with too many seasons ... spread thinly, with lots of fillers.

And about those "silver linings" you're fond of. They're a bit like finding a single M&M in a bag of trail mix. How about tossing a couple more into the blend?

In the spirit of constructive feedback, Universe ... I'm not asking for a rewrite, just a few edits. Less tragedy, more comedy. Less "trial by fire," more "walk in the park."

And maybe ... just maybe ... a few less moments that feel like I'm in a hidden-camera prank show where the joke's always on me.

Perhaps sprinkle in a few more ordinary days filled with speedy internet and good hair.

Thank you!

xo, Karen

Writing this humorous "Complaint Letter to the Universe" felt so healing and freeing ... that I encourage you to write your own!

Next up—here's my final tool.

Survival Mode Tool #5: Turning Your Pain into Purpose

They say, "When life gives you lemons, make lemonade." But what if life skips the lemons and just starts chucking boulders at you? What then?

You gather those boulders of pain, toss them in a blender (a metaphorical one—unless you've got a very robust appliance), and turn them into stepping stones. Next, you use these stepping stones to pave a nice path for other folks to follow.

I call this turning your pain into a legacy project!

Every disaster, every heartbreak, every monumental screw-up—these aren't just personal failings. They're educational material to help someone else.

So share what you've learned via a book, a podcast, a movie, a coaching practice, a course, a nonprofit—or just have a meaningful conversation at a coffee shop.

You've earned a degree from the School of Hard Knocks. Put it to good use.

You'll be crafting a legacy—arming others with your knowledge of how to dodge the bullets you couldn't avoid. Because if life is a battle (and it can be), it's better to go into it with some intel from someone who's already been on the front lines. Your disasters and mistakes can be someone else's road map.

Make something productive out of what felt destructive.

It's generous, really—taking all that pain . . . the very worst moments of your life . . . and using all of this to light up the dark corners of someone else's world.

Now, not all legacy projects are born from pain. There's a range of sources you can use to create a legacy project—plus lots of reasons why you should.

Your legacy project could spring from your talents, your passions, your skills, and your inexplicable love of whatever it is you love. So, coming up next we're gonna dive into the variety of ways you can create your legacy project—as well as the big why.

24

THE PURPOSE OF LIFE IS TO FIND AND DO THE PURPOSE OF YOUR LIFE

You know that expression "The more things change, the more they stay the same"?

Well, Aristotle said it first—but he said it in his own particular style.

Aristotle believed that the universe is in a state of constant motion—always changing, always evolving. However, there's one thing that never wavers: what he called "entelechy"—your unique-to-you highest potential. It's always there—waiting for you to tap into it.

Aristotle believed that every living thing on this planet comes preloaded with its own entelechy—its unique potential seed for becoming its truest, fullest self.

Consider the mighty oak tree.

Its journey to greatness begins with a small acorn seed (aka its entelechy).

Of course, this seed has to go through certain stages of development in order to reach its full potential. But the organism's full potential remains a constant. In the case of the acorn seed—it's to become a mighty oak tree. You will never see an acorn seed become a petunia plant, an umbrella, or a pizza.

Just like that acorn, you've got your own entelechy.

Some people refer to this "inner potential seed" as "your true calling."

Aristotle called it your "specific function." (Pssst . . . in Greek, it's "ergon.")

Either way, it's the thing inside you that pulls you toward what you were meant to be and do.

Aristotle believed you need to take time to nourish your unique seed, so you can grow into your mightiest oak self. Otherwise you risk ending up as a stunted bonsai.

But Aristotle didn't stop there. He argued that growing your seed isn't enough. You've got to use it to help the world, contributing to what he called "the greater good."

What's the greater good?

It means you're not just looking out for number one, but for numbers two through seven billion. You're caring about the collective well-being of humanity.

According to Aristotle, each of us has a unique role to play in this world. But he wasn't simply talking about getting a job and earning an income. He was spotlighting a far nobler task: taking your unique inner potential, and using it to help others.

Because, frankly, the world could really use your entelechy's help!

If you manage to do both—grow yourself and serve others—you'll activate mighty oak status—and feel truly fulfilled.

Aristotle's philosophies around entelechy are backed by a few modern-day studies.

Consider the research paper "The Ideal Road Not Taken" by Tom Gilovich and Shai Davidai. These guys dove deep into the tangled web of human regrets and discovered something interesting.

Most regrets fall into three categories:
- The stuff you *should* have done (your "ought-to self")
- The mundane, everyday mistakes you make because you're human (your "actual self")
- The big, bold dreams you *could* have chased but didn't (your "ideal self")

Guess what? A whopping 72 percent of people's regrets were tied to that third category—the ideal self. Not chasing dreams. Not stepping into one's full potential. In other words, ignoring one's entelechy.

When I read this study, I thought, *Hey, Aristotle was onto this exact thing centuries ago.* Gilovich and Davidai just gave it a new coat of paint.

Next, let's pivot to something called "ikigai."

This is a Japanese philosophy that encourages you to blend your strongest passions and talents with a mission to help the world.

The four pillars of ikigai are:
1. What you love
2. What you're good at
3. What the world needs
4. What you can be paid to do

When you balance all four, you hit the jackpot: a life that feels meaningful.

Aristotle would have liked *ikigai*—except he didn't require your "specific function" to be tied to money. But otherwise, ikigai and Aristotle are on the same page: Figure out what you're good at and use it to serve others.

This idea—of rolling up your sleeves and doing some good in the world—isn't new or rare. It's a timeless belief, repeated throughout history.

Pretty much all religions and spiritual practices preach the importance of living a life of service.
- **Christianity:** Being of service is called "diakonia." It's all about living your faith actively through loving actions.
- **Buddhism:** "Dana" is a practice that encourages being of service. This is a gentle nudge to let go of possessions, dissolve the ego, and deepen your connection to others.
- **Judaism:** Being of service is known as "tikkun olam," meaning "repairing the world." A reminder that through conscious effort, everyone can help make the world better, one act of kindness at a time.
- **Islam:** "Zakat" is one of five pillars and involves giving a portion of your wealth to the needy, supporting the community.

Plus countless influential thinkers have recommended being of service.
- Martin Luther King Jr. said, "Life's most persistent and urgent question is, 'What are you doing for others?'"
- Dalai Lama said, "Our prime purpose in this life is to help others. And if you can't help them, at least don't hurt them."

- Maya Angelou said, "I've learned that you shouldn't go through life with a catcher's mitt on both hands; you need to be able to throw something back."
- Anne Frank said, "How wonderful it is that nobody need wait a single moment before starting to improve the world."

So, whether you're listening to old voices or modern researchers, the message is clear:

The goal of life isn't to become the richest person in the cemetery. It's to figure out what you're good at—and use it to do good in the world. That's where the biggest fulfillment is found.

Why does being of service feel so darn good?

I have a few theories.

1. In chapter 8, I explained that one of the secrets of true happiness (eudaimonia) is to live a soul-directed life—not ego-directed, wallet-directed, or lust-directed. You gotta prioritize actions your soul can be proud of, because in a way the soul is your G-spot for happiness. When you're being of service, it's like a shot of adrenaline straight to your soul.
2. We're social creatures—crafted from the same essence as anthills and beehives. We need the pack. We thrive on connections. Helping others reinforces our bonds and gives us a sense of belonging. In a way, it's not just about feeling good. It's about feeling connected and necessary. When we're helping others, our "thrive switch" is flipped to the "on" position.
3. When you're being of service, you feel like you're here on this planet for a reason. And we humans need meaning and purpose to feel engaged in our lives—to feel like our existence matters. It's the difference between floating adrift in the sea of life versus paddling your boat with a sense of direction.

This brings me to an interesting theory from Carl Jung.

Jung is that famous Swiss psychiatrist (from the early 1900s) who wouldn't just listen to you rant about your ex. Instead, he'd point out the patterns of your rants, helping you to see the "why" behind your feelings.

If your subconscious had a spokesperson . . . it would be Carl Jung.

Anyway, Jung believed that we humans need a high-level spiritual quest in our lives—a pursuit that gives us a feeling of meaning and purpose. If we don't have high-level quests, we'll try to fill that void with low-level spiritual quests—in the form of addictions, drama, conflict, or any unhealthy or self-destructive habit.

Why do we go there? Because, as Jung figured, a little chaos is far better than being bored out of your mind. Basically, Jung viewed low-level spiritual quests as your backup plan—when you don't have a mightier higher purpose. These lower-level quests serve as tragic consolation prizes to help you to feel like your life has something important to focus on—even if it's a lousy focus.

But because lower-level quests don't contribute to your personal development, they never fulfill you. They're like junk food for the soul. They leave you feeling empty and emotionally unnourished.

The solution?

Jung believed that you can more readily dump your negative low-level spiritual quests by intentionally developing high-level spiritual quests—finding a driving positive force that propels you forward.

Yes, Jung was convinced that if you're stuck in a cycle of not-so-great habits, you can stop this pattern by chasing more high-level stuff. The big dreams. The pursuits that really matter.

But here's the thing: You can't stop your bad patterns simply by busying yourself with random distractions. You need a high-level quest—something meaningful that matters to YOU-ier you. Otherwise you won't fill that void inside you.

Jung called this pursuit "self-actualization"—which was his Jungian term for all the ancient rants by Aristotle to focus on growing into your best self.

Plus, what Jung called a "high-level spiritual quest" is pretty much what Aristotle called your "specific function."

So these two brilliant minds were very much in agreement. They both believed that in order to live a truly fulfilling life, you must find that thing that makes you say, "Yeah, this is why I'm here on this planet!"

Maybe for you that means working at a dog shelter. But for someone else it's about diving into charity work, penning that novel, or kicking off a podcast.

Whatever it is, it's gotta be something that genuinely makes the world a bit brighter—while also being in alignment with your YOU-iest "specific function."

Since this book is all about the gifts of death awareness, I'm going to share how being of service isn't just a beautiful thing—it can also be your legacy project.

WHAT IS A LEGACY PROJECT?

It's your profound, indelible mark on the world—your contribution. It's what lingers when you're gone, in the minds and hearts of others. It's your loving message to the world that says, "I was here, and I made a difference."

Plus, it's also that thing that when you do it, you feel the way Joan of Arc felt when she famously said, "I am not afraid . . . I was born to do this."

By the way, when Joan said this famous line, she wasn't just hyped up on medieval energy drinks. No, Joan was riding high on feeling like she was fully embracing her entelechy, her specific function, her ikigai, her high-level spiritual quest, her self-actualization. Because she was doing what she knew she was good at—while doing good in the world.

So when Joan said she was born to do this, she was essentially saying:

"Leading in the Hundred Years' War? Yeah, that's my legacy project!"

The good news:

Your legacy project doesn't need to be as big as leading a resistance movement. You just need to tap into your unique strengths to help others. And it's not about the size of your audience. It's about the depth of your impact.

Your legacy could be found in those late-night talks with a friend who needed advice. Or it could be the mentorship you gave to a rookie in your field. Meaning? It can simply be about moments when you chose kindness. And yes, this even includes those small moments with strangers—giving up your subway seat, sharing your umbrella, holding the elevator door.

There Are Basically Three Kinds of Legacy Projects, and They Often Overlap
1. Human-to-Human Legacy

These are your people-fueled continuance. Often they are what you pass on to your kids, grandkids, nieces, nephews, spiritual kids, stepkids, the whole family, friends, work colleagues, random person-in-need kinda shebang. It's the legacy you leave when you teach helpful stuff to someone who's struggling. It could be the big things like self-love and resilience. Or it could be how to set up a website or make a decent omelet. Or it could be offering career tips or networking intros. It's passing on your YOU-iest wisdom—person-to-person.

2. Community and Global Legacy

This is when you decide, perhaps during a sleepless night, that you're going to do something to make the world slightly better. Take, for instance, the idea of donating food to people in need. Maybe getting involved in a global clean-water project. Or even creating a cleanup event in your community.

3. Brainchild Legacy

This is an intellectual or creative legacy—where you paint, write, code, invent, or create something that helps people in some way. This could be a book where you turn your pain into purpose—and share what you learned to help others. Or it could be a well-crafted birdhouse or a geeky tech product you develop to connect volunteers to places they're needed most. The point is: You brainstormed an idea to help others—and you made it real.

Your legacy project doesn't need to be huge and flashy. You don't need to put in a million dollars or a million hours or help a million people!

A Legacy Project Could Be as Simple as . . .
- Mentoring someone
- Starting a scholarship
- Volunteering at—or donating to—a charity
- Coaching a Little League team
- Pouring your love into an amazing lasagna recipe—to be savored by generations to come
- Doing anything that sends positive ripples into the world—saying, "I was here, and I gave a damn."

I want to emphasize again: ALL ripples count—no matter their size.
You don't need to be making tsunami waves to make a difference. In fact,

sometimes it's those small ripples—with just a few people—that last the longest and matter most.

In the words of Mother Teresa: "If you want to change the world, go home and love your family."

Think about it. Maybe you just help one person—but then that person's life changes for the better. Boom! Deep fulfillment activated!

Or maybe that one person you helped passes on your inspiration to someone else—who then passes it on to someone else—*and so on*. As a result, your one-on-one ripples don't stay one-on-one for long. They wind up echoing through time.

So don't sweat it if you're not ending world hunger while juggling flaming swords. All ripples count. Because even the smallest change can set off a chain reaction that keeps rolling . . . *long after you're gone*.

The best legacies, the ones that really stick, come down to this:

- Did you step up when someone needed you?
- Did you make someone's life better?
- Did you leave the world a little better than you found it?

Now here's the cherry on top:

When you're of service, you get something back when you give. It's like the universe has this weird math—where the more you help others, the richer your own life becomes.

These aren't just poetic words. This is a research-backed fact.

Dr. Koichiro Shiba, a researcher at Boston University, studied over 13,000 people and found a big win for the do-gooders. It turns out that having a sense of purpose (because you're out there being of service) doesn't just bump up your happiness stats. It also significantly reduces your risk of premature death.

Dr. Shiba found:

- Those people who wake up feeling like they're doing something that matters? They face only a 15.2 percent risk of dying prematurely.
- Meanwhile, the folks who feel like "Why am I even here?" face a much bigger mortality risk—one that's as high as 36.5 percent!

That's more than double!

Meaning?

If you know WHY you're waking up in the morning, you'll actually keep waking up for more mornings!

Best of all . . .

Enjoying a fulfilling legacy project will not only empower you to live longer. It will help you to live wider and fuller. You'll feel more alive while you are here.

The ultimate lesson: The purpose of your life is to find and do the purpose of your life!

Discover your WHY for being here. Make your WHY your legacy project—and make a difference in the world. If you can do this, then you'll be making "Deathbed You" happy and proud. Because in the end, you're not going to care about how many throw pillows you owned—or how many craft cocktails you Instagrammed. You're going to care about how you impacted the world and the people around you.

So make sure you're pursuing a life that doesn't merely fill up time—but fills you up, and fills up others too—because you're doing something that matters!

Let's Brainstorm Your Legacy Project.

It's time to find that thing that makes you feel like your time here mattered—like you planted a weird little flag in the ground that future generations might trip over and think, "Huh, someone actually cared about this world."

Here's how to find that flag-worthy thing:

Reflect on your peak moments: Think about times when you didn't just feel alive, you felt *ALIVE-alive*. What were you doing? Who were you with? These moments are a breadcrumb trail to your purpose—your legacy project.

Reflect on your lowest lows: Explore how you can morph your pain into purpose and help others. Try to view your pain not simply as a wound, but as in invitation to teach.

Consider when you lose track of time: Psychologist Mihaly Csikszentmihalyi *(don't worry, no one knows how to pronounce it)* calls this "being in flow." What are your flow zones? Your "why" might be hidden there. If it's working in your garden, you may want to volunteer at a community garden. If it's balancing your monthly household budget, you may want to teach financial literacy.

Explore what you can't stop talking about: Listen to your rants. The issues that ignite your fiercest debates and most passionate speeches. These are clues to what matters to you. And what matters to you is tied to your "why."

Look at what irritates you: Sometimes, your "why" hides in your frustrations. For instance, if disorganization drives you crazy, perhaps your "why" revolves around creating order and improving systems. Not just for your own personal benefit, but to leave a legacy of efficiency for others. So, reflect on your whining—and consider how overcoming your frustrations can contribute to a legacy that makes you feel proud.

HOW TO GET STARTED

Next up . . . how do you ensure your legacy project doesn't just linger in the Land of Wishful Thinking?

After all . . . making changes in your life is admittedly scary. Inside you there's a voice that whispers, "Stay here—it's easier." But ease is a sly companion. It lulls you into a false sense of contentment, where nothing grows . . . except perhaps a growing sense of "Why didn't I?"

It's your choice . . .

- You can drift along . . . carried forward by the current of easy gratification.
- Or you can mindfully swim against this powerful tide . . . toward something that truly matters. Yeah, this is the tougher choice. It demands more from you. But the payoff? It's not even in the same league. It's the difference between living by accident . . . and living on purpose.

So I'm hoping you gather up your courage to make that leap—and start pursuing your legacy project.

Here are some tools to help.

TOOL 1: FIND YOUR "WHY"

Viktor Frankl (as mentioned, an incredibly brilliant psychologist who survived the Holocaust) is known for famously saying:

"He who has a why to live for can bear almost any how."

Meaning? The more you know your "why" for doing something that's challenging—the more your "how" becomes manageable.

Why power = the strongest willpower.

For example:

- Let's say you tell yourself, "I want to get fit." That's fine. It's not bad.
- But now try, "I want to get fit so I can play with my kids without feeling like an asthmatic penguin!" Suddenly, you're not just exercising. You're on a mission.

Here Are Potential WHYs for Your Legacy Project—or Brainstorm Your Own.

1. **Why? To inspire youth:** I'm setting up programs to help young people tackle life head-on, aiming to shape a generation that's ready to lead and make wiser choices.
2. **Why? To improve people's health:** I'm starting a community garden to not only beautify our neighborhood but to also encourage everyone to eat fresh and live healthier.
3. **Why? To spread knowledge:** I'm writing a book about bouncing back from tough times, hoping to show others that it's possible to find light, even in the darkest places.
4. **Why? To encourage entrepreneurship:** I'm starting a mentorship program to equip budding entrepreneurs with the same tools that helped me to climb the success ladder—so I can help others to build ladders that they can climb too.
5. **Why? To champion equality:** I'm pushing for equal rights, hoping to help forge a world where everyone, no matter their background, has a fair chance to succeed.

Plus Here Are Some WHYs Based on Smaller (but Still Very Beautiful) Ripples...

1. **Why? To spread kindness:** I want to commit to doing one kind act each day, whether it's helping a neighbor with groceries or complimenting a stranger, to bring a little more light into someone's day.

2. **Why? To support others:** I plan to set aside a small amount of money each month for charity, because even the smallest contribution can help someone in need.

3. **Why? To encourage positivity:** I aim to be nicer to everyone I meet — so I can help people who are struggling to feel happier—plus make my community a friendlier place, one interaction at a time.

Get curious about your WHY and use it like your personal cheerleader! Whenever you're thinking, "I can't do this," repeat your WHY—and you'll feel more empowered to keep going.

Bonus Tip: Your WHY Is Usually Linked to Your Favorite Core Values.
So you should craft your WHY into a motivational "I am and so I do" statement—then slap it onto your To-Die List.

For example:

I am (empathically loving) and so I (set aside eleven dollars on the eleventh day of each month to give to a charity).

Warning: There will be many times you'll want to quit your legacy project.

Maybe you'll feel fear, lack faith, or won't want to risk ridicule. If this happens, I encourage you to use the following tool, which deploys mortality awareness as the ultimate procrastination killer.

TOOL 2: DEATHBED MEDITATION

Imagine this: You're at the end of your life, you're reflecting, and you realize, holy smokes, I did that amazing thing that helped someone (or many ones)! You're proud of the risks you took, the courage it required.

Death Bed Meditations are a powerful reminder:

If you're not committing to something bigger than your comfort zone, you're not fully living . . . you're just skimming the surface of your life.

So, when doubt pulls up a chair, when quitting whispers sweet promises about safety and ease, stop. Take a breath. Picture yourself in that final bed, your body still, your mind full.

- You're feeling happy that you helped someone think in new ways.
- You're smiling knowing you made someone feel less alone in this crazy, mixed-up world.
- You're experiencing true fulfillment—because your life made it a little easier for someone else.

You must seize the day—because that's the only way to seize your life!

With this in mind, you should seize this mortality awareness quote by writer Erma Bombeck: "When I stand before God at the end of my life, I would hope that I would not have a single bit of talent left, and could say, I used everything you gave me."

I love Erma for saying that! Plus I gotta say—she sure stamped her "Was Here!" sticker on my brain and heart. I remember reading Erma when I was younger and thinking, "I want to write funny, inspiring books like her someday!"

Listen up: Here's what I want you to carry with you when this book is done.

When you're on your deathbed, it won't be the awards or the "first place in whatever" that you'll treasure most. It will be remembering how someone once told you, "You know that thing you said that one time? It really changed things for me."

These are the moments that will coax a smile from you—even when you're surrounded by all those weird hospital gadgets. Knowing you connected with people. Shared something deep and real. Those are the kind of memories that will matter most.

So, if at the end, you've managed to pass on some life lessons—or shared a part of yourself that helped someone to cope with life's ups and downs—then you've crafted a legacy worth claiming.

Imagine if Everybody Lived with This Kind of End Goal in Mind

If only more people didn't simply prioritize feeling good (aka hedonia).

If only more people focused on being a good human—someone who strives to bring more good into the world (aka eudaimonia).

If only more people harnessed their talents and skills not for ego-directed reasons (aka hedonia).

If only more people did so for soul-directed reasons—to be a positive force that makes a positive echo in the world (aka eudaimonia).

If each of us did a little more of that ... imagine the kind of wonderful world we'd live in—and leave behind.

My hope for you:

On that distant, inevitable day, when you're propped up on a pile of pillows and the ticking of the room's generic wall clock becomes strangely significant ... you can smile knowing that you were someone who made the most of your singular shot at life.

You understood that you didn't need to leave behind a pyramid or a statue. You could leave behind something far better. A little part of yourself that continues to inspire others to live at their best, to thrive and grow into their highest-potential mighty oak selves.

Remember how, at the beginning of this book, I wrote about how stars keep sparkling in the sky long after they've burned out? Well, you've got the same option when you pass on too.

That enduring echo of light stars leave behind ... it's not so different from the legacy that you can leave behind. Yes, you too have the potential to keep shining—to leave a mark that persists after you're long gone.

All you have to do is craft a legacy that doesn't merely say, "I was here." A legacy that also adds, "and I learned a lot along the way—and shared a lot too."

THE END
Well, that's it for this book.
Your life? Still very much a work in progress—with more to be written.
Now go out there and make some ripples and waves!

Acknowledgments

In this small space, big thanks are due.

To the Circle Close to Home (The Ones Not Already in the Dedication): Bonnie Ault, who sacrificed precious Netflix time to read drafts—including endless revisions. To my truth-tellers and dream-holders who mastered the art of "loving feedback": Dana-Maxx Pomerantz, Phyllis Leibowitz, Robin Gorman-Newman, Jennifer Hill, Kristine Carlson, Gayle Stacher, Jason Abrams, Arielle Ford, and Lindsay Kriger.

To My Living-Fully Guides: Safije Alija, Berrnadette Penotti, Meri Frischman, Bonnie Winston, Elise Museles, Josselyne Herman-Saccio, Alexa Fischer, Lindsey Biel, Li Saul, Laura Smith, Susan Gorka—and many more. You showed me what it means to live with meaning and purpose. Plus, a special thank you to the beautiful-hearted Frank V. DeAndrea Jr., who came into my life after my father's passing, as a gift from my dad to me, wrapped in synchronicity.

To the Book Whisperers: Esther Blum, who heard my wild idea about death awareness and instead of backing away slowly, pulled out a map and said, "I know exactly where to send this idea." Dalyn Miller, my literary matchmaker (aka agent); Rick Chillot, who polished my words until they sparkled without losing their soul. And to the entire team at BenBella Publishing who took a chance on making death awareness actually sound fun: Susan Welte, Sarah Avinger, Leah Wilson, Monica Lowry, Jennifer Canzoneri, Alicia Kania, Adrienne Lang, Ariel Jewett, Rachel Phares, Madeline Grigg, Isabelle Rubio, Brigid Pearson, Lindsay Marshall, and Heather Butterfield.

To My Client Heroes: I appreciate all you brave souls who tested these ideas in real time, who proved that mortality awareness isn't just theory but actually life-changing.

If this book throws any light into the world, it's because each of you helped kindle the flame.

About the Author

Karen Salmansohn is a bestselling author (with over 2 million books and courses sold), a leading Behavioral Change Expert, a columnist for Oprah.com and *Psychology Today*, and a thought leader on social media with a following of 1.5 million fans worldwide (including folks like Deepak Chopra, Tony Robbins, Jon Stewart, Gretchen Rubin, Tim Ferris, Sharon Salzberg, Marie Forleo, Tony Hsieh, Arianna Huffington). Karen's known for pioneering "self-help for people who wouldn't be caught dead doing self-help," transforming the genre with bestsellers like *How To Be Happy Dammit*. Now, at 64, she's spearheading the Mortality Awareness Movement, showing how death awareness can be a powerful catalyst for living more fully. She offers free resources, articles, courses and coaching at NotSalmon.com and YourToDieForLife.com.